Canadian Citizenship Made Easy

A Study Guide in Simple English

By Drew Smith

Publishing services provided by  Archangel Ink

ISBN: 1519121296

ISBN-13: 978-1519121295

Canadian Citizenship Made Easy is a study guide for the Canadian Citizenship Exam. All of the information you need to pass the Citizenship Exam is found in this book. ***Canadian Citizenship Made Easy*** uses simple, easy–to–understand English to help you prepare for the exam. Each chapter is followed by Multiple-Choice questions and some optional review questions for discussion.

Please visit www.beavermaple.ca for more citizenship preparation.

Table of Contents

Chapter 1

BEING A CANADIAN

As a new Canadian, you will have many rights and responsibilities to uphold. These rights and responsibilities come from Canada's unique heritage and law. The laws of Canada come from many sources. English common law, France's civil code, and Great Britain's constitution are all sources and influences. Canada's federal and provincial governments have also made laws.

In the year 1215, the Magna Carta (the Great Charter) was signed in England. Some important freedoms that Canadians still embrace today come from this old document. They include:

The freedom of association

The freedom of thought, belief, opinion, and expression (this includes freedom of speech and freedom of the press)

The freedom of peaceful assembly

The freedom of conscience and religion

Canada also recognizes *habeas corpus*, which means anyone is allowed to question "unlawful detention."

The Rights of a Canadian Citizen

In **1982**, Canada amended (or fixed) its constitution by passing the **Constitution Act**. With this act, Canada added the **Canadian Charter of Rights and Freedoms** to its constitution. The Charter outlines the freedoms and rights of Canadians. The most important rights are:

Mobility Rights – Canadians can work and live anywhere in Canada.

Aboriginal Peoples' Rights – The Charter recognizes the rights of Aboriginal people in Canada.

Official Language Rights and Minority Language Education Rights – All federal services must be offered in both French and English. Canadians have the right to educate their children in either French or English no matter where they live in Canada. **English and French are the two official languages of Canada.**

Multiculturalism – Multiculturalism is an important part of Canada's heritage and present–day culture.

John Buchan was the Governor General of Canada between 1935 and 1940. He believed that all immigrant groups should try to keep their own identity, so that together, all immigrant groups will make a unique national identity. Buchan was an early supporter of multiculturalism.

The Responsibilities of Canadian Citizenship

All Canadians must assume the following responsibilities:

Obey the Law – All people, businesses, and governments must respect and follow the law in Canada. When immigrants come to Canada they are expected to follow Canada's rule of law.

Take Responsibility for Oneself and One's Family – As an individual, you must work hard to support yourself and your family. This is an important value in Canadian society.

Serve on a Jury – If you are selected, you must serve on a jury.

Vote in Elections – You need to vote in municipal, provincial (or territorial), and federal elections.

Help Other People in Your Community – There are many different ways and places you can volunteer in Canada.

Protect Canada's Environment and Heritage – All citizens need to think about Canada's future and help protect and sustain Canada's beautiful nature and important heritage.

THE CANADIAN FORCES

The military (navy, army, and air force) in Canada is called the **Canadian Forces.** In Canada, you do not have to serve in the military. However, the Canadian Forces is a great career opportunity for those who want to help defend Canada. You can also volunteer in the Coast Guard, your local police force, or your local fire department.

In Canada's north, a special part of the Canadian Forces called the **Canadian Rangers** help keep Canada's north secure and safe.

Multiple-Choice Questions – Chapter 1

1. What sources do the laws of Canada come from?

    a) English common law

    b) France's civil code

    c) Great Britain's constitution

    d) All of the above

2. What is a freedom that Canadians do *not* enjoy?

    a) Freedom of peaceful assembly

    b) Freedom of conscience and religion

    c) Freedom to carry weapons

    d) Freedom of association

3. What was added to the Canadian Constitution in 1982?

    a) The Quebec Act

    b) The Treaty of Versailles

    c) The Canadian Charter of Rights and Freedoms

    d) The North American Free Trade Agreement

4. What are mobility rights?

    a) The right to leave and enter Canada anytime

    b) The right to move to any province

    c) The right to work anywhere in Canada

    d) All of the above

5. What freedom or right is not included in the Canadian Charter of Rights and Freedoms?

    a) Aboriginal Peoples' Rights

    b) Discrimination Rights

    c) Official Language Rights

    d) Multiculturalism

6. What are the official languages of Canada?

    a) English and in some situations French

    b) English, French, and Inuktitut

    c) English, French, and the Aboriginal languages

    d) English and French

7. Are immigrants expected to follow the laws of Canada?

    a) Yes

    b) No

    c) Yes, but only if they do not conflict with their own cultural beliefs

    d) Sometimes

8. What is not an example of a responsibility a Canadian must assume?

    a) Serving on a jury

    b) Voting in elections

    c) Helping people in your community

    d) Joining the military

9. What statement is true?

    a) Judges are above the law

    b) No one is above the law

    c) The RCMP have special privileges within the laws of Canada

    d) The Prime Minister cannot be arrested

10. What is the name of the military in Canada?

    a) The Canadian Federal Police

    b) The Canadian Forces

    c) The Toronto Maple Leafs

    d) The Royal Canadian Mounted Police

11. Is military service mandatory in Canada?

    a) No

    b) Yes

    c) Only for men

    d) Only for students between the ages of 18 and 20

12. Who helps keep Canada's north safe?

    a) The O.P.P.

    b) The Hamilton Tiger–Cats

    c) The Canadian Rangers

    d) The Nunavut Tundra Patrol

Review Questions – Chapter 1

1. What are three freedoms a Canadian enjoys?

2. What great Charter was signed in 1215?

3. What is *habeas corpus*?

4. What act was signed in 1982?

5. What are three rights that are included in the Canadian Charter of Rights and Freedoms?

6. What does multiculturalism mean?

7. What are five responsibilities a Canadian has?

8. Is voting mandatory in Canada?

9. What are the three components of the Canadian Forces?

10. Why do you think Canada has a special group to protect the north?

Chapter 2

THE PEOPLE OF CANADA

Canada, which is also known as ***the Great Dominion***, is the only **constitutional monarchy** in North America.

Canadians celebrate the words "**Peace, Order, and Good Government.**" These words come from **the British North America Act of 1867**, which formed the Confederation of Canada (the birth of Canada). Even though the birth year of Canada is 1867, the history and heritage of the Canadian people started long before that.

There are three founding peoples of Canada:

1. **Aboriginal Peoples**
2. **The French**
3. **The British**

The Aboriginal Peoples

Thousands of years ago, people migrated across the Bering Strait (which was an ice bridge at the time) to populate the Americas. The Aboriginal people are descendants of these early inhabitants. Aboriginal groups lived in what is now called Canada for thousands of years before the first European explorers came to the Americas.

In 1763, King George III of the United Kingdom made a royal proclamation (an announcement) which gave territorial rights to Aboriginal Peoples. There are three main groups of aboriginal peoples:

First Nations (formerly called Indians) – The First Nations make up 65 percent of all Aboriginal peoples in Canada.

Inuit – Most Inuit people live in the Arctic and speak the language Inuktitut. Inuit means *the People* in Inuktitut. The Inuit make up 4 percent of all Aboriginal peoples in Canada.

Metis – The Metis are a people of both European and Aboriginal descent. Metis either speak English, French, or their own language called Michif. The Metis represent 30 percent of all Aboriginal peoples in Canada.

For nearly two hundred years, until 1980, the government of Canada put many Aboriginal children in residential schools. The government thought that it would be better for Aboriginal children to learn English and to learn Canadian culture. Unfortunately, many children suffered abuse in these schools, and in 2008, the government apologized to all former students.

THE FRENCH AND THE BRITISH

In Canada, there are 7 million **Francophones** (French speakers). Most of them live in Quebec, but many Francophones also live in Ontario, Manitoba, and New Brunswick. **The only officially bilingual province in Canada is New Brunswick.**

THE ACADIAN PEOPLE

In 1604, immigrants from France began colonizing the east coast of Canada in what are now called the Maritime provinces (New Brunswick, Nova Scotia, and Prince Edward Island). The descendants of these early French immigrants are called **the Acadians**.

THE GREAT UPHEAVAL

Between 1755 and 1763, there was a war between Britain and France that resulted in many Acadians being forced to leave Canada. Some Acadians went to France and others went to the United States of America. This period in Canadian history is called the **Great Upheaval**. Some Acadians remained in Canada and their culture is alive and well in the Maritime provinces.

THE QUEBECERS

The people of Quebec are called the **Quebecers**. Most people in Quebec speak French, but there are also one million English speakers living there. These English speakers are also called Anglo–Quebecers. In 2006, the government of Canada acknowledged that the Quebecois are "a nation within Canada."

ANGLOPHONES

English–speaking Canadians, or Anglophones, are mostly descended from early English, Scottish, Irish, and Welsh settlers who came to Canada starting in the 1600s.

Even though most Canadians were born in Canada, Canada is still known throughout the world as being *the land of immigrants*.

DIVERSITY IN CANADA

Canada has two official languages: English and French. Besides English or French, there are many nonofficial languages spoken throughout Canada. After English and French, Chinese languages are the most commonly spoken.

Most Canadians are Christians, and the most popular type of Christianity practiced is Catholicism.

Gay and lesbian marriages are recognized and are legal under Canadian law.

Multiple-Choice Questions – Chapter 2

1. What is Canada also known as?

    a) The Great White North

    b) The Great Dominion

    c) The Northern Territories

    d) Prince Rupert's Land

2. What Act formed the Confederation of Canada?

    a) The British North America Act of 1887

    b) The Quebec Act of 1774

    c) The British North America Act of 1867

    d) The Constitution Act of 1982

3. Who are the three founding peoples of Canada?

    a) French, British, and Vikings

    b) First Nations, Inuit, and Metis

    c) Acadian, French, and Aboriginal

    d) Aboriginal, French, and British

4. Where did the Canadian government put many Aboriginal children from the 1800s until the 1980s?

    a) Reserves

    b) Residential schools

    c) The Northern Territories

    d) Larger municipalities

5. What are the three main groups of Aboriginal peoples in Canada?

   a) First Nations, Inuit, and Acadian

   b) Algonquin, Dene, and Inuit

   c) Inuit, Metis, and First Nations

   d) Acadian, Inuit, and Metis

6. What is the smallest group of Aboriginal Peoples in Canada?

   a) Inuit

   b) First Nations

   c) Metis

7. What is the only officially bilingual province in Canada?

   a) Ontario

   b) Quebec

   c) New Brunswick

   d) Nova Scotia

8. Who are the Acadians?

   a) An ethnic group that resides in British Columbia

   b) Descendants of early French settlers

   c) English–speaking Quebecers

   d) A group of people descended from early Norse settlers

9. Who are the Quebecers?

   a) The people of Quebec

   b) Francophones

   c) Anglophones

   d) Acadians

10. What is an Anglophone?

    a) A person who speaks English as a second language

    b) A French speaker

    c) A bilingual person

    d) A person who speaks English as a first language

11. What is the largest religious denomination in Canada?

    a) Muslim

    b) Catholic

    c) Protestant

    d) Sikh

12 After English and French, what language(s) are spoken the most in Canada?

    a) Spanish

    b) Arabic

    c) Chinese languages

    d) Punjabi

Review Questions – Chapter 2

1. What are three important words that come from the British North America Act of 1867 that Canadians like to celebrate?

2. Why does the history and heritage of Canada start before 1867?

3. What were some of the problems with the residential school program?

4. Who gave Aboriginal people territorial rights in 1763?

5. How many Francophones live in Canada?

6. What was the Great Upheaval?

7. Do all Quebecers speak French?

8. From which settlers are most English–speaking Canadians descended?

9. Why is Canada called *the land of immigrants*?

10. Are gay and lesbian marriages legally recognized in Canada?

Chapter 3

THE HISTORY OF CANADA

Before Europeans came to Canada, there were many different Aboriginal groups living in all parts of the country. Each Aboriginal group was different in language and culture, and quite often, different groups went to war against each other.

The lives of the Aboriginal people changed when Europeans started to come and settle in Canada. When Europeans first saw the Aboriginal people, they called them "Indians," thinking that they were in the East Indies. Even though many groups of Aboriginal people made alliances with Europeans, many died from the diseases that the Europeans brought with them to Canada.

THE FIRST EUROPEAN CONTACT

The first Europeans to reach Canada were the Vikings (also called the Norsemen) over 1,000 years ago. However, the Vikings didn't stay long in Canada. They only stayed for a short while. There is a famous archaeological site called *L'Anse aux Meadows* in Newfoundland where you can see the remains of a Viking settlement.

EARLY EXPLORERS

John Cabot, who was an Italian living in England, came to what is now called Newfoundland in **1497** and claimed the land for England. Cabot was also the first person to draw a map of Canada's east coast.

Jacques Cartier was a French explorer who came to Canada three times between 1534 and 1542. Cartier claimed the new land for the king of France, King Francis I.

On one of his trips, Cartier heard someone use the Iroquoian word ***kanata***, which meant *village*. Historians are not exactly sure what happened, but most believe that Cartier misunderstood the real meaning of the word *kanata* and thought it meant the whole land, not just the village. After this experience, the name *Canada* started to be used on maps.

French explorer Samuel de Champlain founded Quebec City in 1608. The French settlements in North America became known as **Royal New France**. The French made alliances with many First Nation groups to help fight the Iroquois. The Iroquois and the French fought for one hundred years until both sides signed a peace treaty in 1701.

Bishop Laval, Jean Talon, and Count Frontenac were famous French leaders in Royal New France.

The Fur Trade

The French needed peace with the Aboriginal groups in Canada because they needed their help to trap and trade beaver fur. Beaver pelts (skins) were worth a lot of money in Europe.

The British were also heavily involved in the Fur Trade. The Hudson's Bay Company was given all of the land around the Hudson Bay in 1670 by King Charles II of England. Many Hudson's Bay Company trading posts such as Fort Garry (Winnipeg) and Fort Victoria (Victoria) went on to become cities.

French traders were the main competition of the Hudson's Bay Company. The French traders and fur transporters became well known for their hard work in a difficult landscape. People started calling them *voyageurs* (Boatmen) and *coureurs des bois* (Woodsmen).

Over time, the British population became bigger than the French population and the two nations fought for control of the land. The most important battle between the two nations happened in **1759** in Quebec City. It was called **the Battle of the Plains of Abraham**. At the end of the battle, the British were victorious. Both the French commander (Marquis de Montcalm) and the British commander (Brigadier James Wolfe) died in the fight. The victory for the British meant that they would control the land in British North America.

Multiple-Choice Questions – Chapter 3

1. Who were the first Europeans to reach Canada?

   a) The Spanish

   b) The French

   c) The British

   d) The Vikings

2. Which explorer was the first to draw a map of Canada's east coast?

   a) King Charles II

   b) Jacques Cartier

   c) John Cabot

   d) Samuel de Champlain

3. What explorer heard the Iroquoian word *kanata*?

   a) Jacques Cartier

   b) Samuel de Champlain

   c) John Cabot

   d) King Charles II

4. Who founded Quebec City in 1608?

   a) Jacques Cartier

   b) John Cabot

   c) John Graves Simcoe

   d) Samuel de Champlain

5. Which two groups made peace in 1701?

    a) The French and the British

    b) The French and the Iroquois

    c) The British and the Huron

    d) The Huron and the Iroquois

6. What were the French settlements in North America called?

    a) Royal New France

    b) Quebec

    c) Stadacona

    d) Acadia

7. What animal was central to the success of the fur trade?

    a) Mink

    b) Fox

    c) Caribou

    d) Beaver

8. What company was granted all of the land around the Hudson Bay to hunt and trade in 1670?

    a) Eaton's

    b) The Hudson's Bay Company

    c) The Quebec Fur exchange

    d) Tim Hortons

9. Who were the *coureur des bois* and the *voyageurs*?

    a) French soldiers

    b) British fur–trading workers

    c) Aboriginal hunters employed by the Hudson's Bay Company

    d) French fur traders and fur transporters

10. What Hudson's Bay Company trading post eventually became Winnipeg?

   a) Fort Niagara

   b) Fort George

   c) Fort Langley

   d) Fort Garry

11. What battle happened in 1759 between the French and the British?

   a) The Battle of the Plains of Abraham

   b) The Battle of Beaver Dams

   c) The Battle of Vimy Ridge

   d) The Battle of Stadacona

12. Which two commanders fought at the Battle of the Plains of Abraham?

   a) Brigadier James Wolfe and Count Frontenac

   b) Brigadier James Wolfe and Marquis de Montcalm

   c) Sir Guy Carleton and the Duke of Wellington

   d) Marquis de Montcalm and Sir Isaac Brock

Review Questions – Chapter 3

1. Who lived in Canada before the first Europeans arrived?

2. Where can you see the remains of a Viking settlement?

3. Who claimed Newfoundland for England in 1497?

4. From which language is the word *kanata*?

5. Who, after fighting for a century, signed a peace treaty in 1701?

6. What was the Fur Trade and why was it so important?

7. Who competed with the Hudson's Bay Company in the Fur Trade?

8. In what city did the Battle of the Plains of Abraham happen?

9. In what year was the Battle of the Plains of Abraham?

10. Who was the French commander at the Battle of the Plains of Abraham?

Chapter 4

AFTER THE PLAINS OF ABRAHAM

Even though the British won the Battle of the Plains of Abraham, they still had to make peace with all of the French people living in Canada. The area where the French people lived was renamed the Province of Quebec. Shortly after, in **1774**, the British passed a law called **the Quebec Act** that allowed the French people to keep their identity and culture. The French were allowed to remain Catholic (the British were Protestants), and they were also allowed to become members of government. The Quebec Act tried to unite the ideas of both British and French law. At this time, the French–speaking Catholics that lived in the Province of Quebec became known as *Canadiens* and *habitants*. Sir Guy Carleton, a Governor of Quebec helped the *Canadiens* keep their rights.

THE AMERICAN REVOLUTION

Just as the dust settled in Quebec, another war broke out to the south. In 1776, the British colonies that were living south of what is now Canada decided to claim independence from Britain.

The United Empire Loyalists (or Loyalists for short) were people living in the revolting British colonies that didn't agree with the revolution, because they still supported the King of England. They remained "loyal" to Britain and instead of fighting against the British, they chose to move northward and come to what is now Canada. More than 40,000 Loyalists of varying ethnic and religious groups came to Nova Scotia and Quebec.

A Mohawk Indian leader named **Joseph Brant** brought thousands of Mohawk Indians with him to Canada. They wanted to support the Crown instead of the American revolutionists.

Since any slave would be a freeman if they fought for the British, more than 3,000 black Loyalists (some were slaves and some were already freedmen) ran away and came to Quebec and Nova Scotia.

British North America

Democracy has a long history in Canada. Representative assemblies were created in late eighteenth century Canada to help govern the provinces fairly.

The first representative assembly of Nova Scotia was in 1758. The first representative assembly of Prince Edward Island was in 1773. The first representative assembly of New Brunswick was in 1785.

In 1791, the British Parliament passed the **Constitutional Act**, which created the English–speaking Upper Canada (which would later become Ontario) and the French–speaking Lower Canada (which would later become Quebec). The Constitutional Act also created legislative assemblies, which consisted of members that were elected by the people.

Before 1867, the area that is now called Canada was called **British North America**. During this time of political growth, British North America also started growing economically. Banks started to open, and a stock exchange in Montreal opened in 1832. The lands of British North America were rich in natural resources such as wood, fish, and animal fur.

THE UNDERGROUND RAILROAD

Lieutenant Governor John Graves Simcoe started to abolish slavery in Upper Canada in 1793, and in 1833, the British Parliament abolished slavery throughout its whole empire. After this, thousands of black slaves escaped to Canada through a secret network called the **Underground Railroad**. Secure routes and safe houses were used to help runaway slaves make their way to British North America.

In 1853, Mary Ann Shadd Cary became the first female publisher in British North America. Her newspaper, called *The Provincial Freeman*, informed people about the antislavery movement and other social issues in Canada and the United States.

Multiple-Choice Questions – Chapter 4

1. After the Battle of the Plains of Abraham, what was the French colony renamed?

   a) Ontario

   b) Province of Quebec

   c) Nova Scotia

   d) Montreal

2. What act in 1774 allowed the French to keep their identity and culture?

   a) The Quebec Act

   b) The Constitutional Act

   c) The British North America Act

   d) The French Constitution Act

3. Who were the *Canadiens* and the *habitants*?

   a) British and French settlers living in Quebec

   b) British settlers living in the new Province of Quebec

   c) Employees of the Fur Trade

   d) The French–speaking Catholics of Quebec

4. Who were the United Empire Loyalists?

   a) Immigrants who left Canada to join the American Revolution

   b) Immigrants who relocated to Ontario from Quebec

   c) Immigrants who remained loyal to Royal New France

   d) Immigrants who came to Canada during the American Revolution because they supported the British Crown

5. How many Loyalists came to Quebec and Nova Scotia during the American Revolution?

    a) About 40,000

    b) About 4,000

    c) About 400,000

    d) About 400

6. Who was Joseph Brant?

    a) A Metis leader

    b) A Mohawk Indian leader

    c) An Inuit leader

    d) A French Canadian leader

7. What did the British Parliament pass in 1791?

    a) The Constitution Act

    b) The Constitutional Act

    c) The Quebec Act

    d) The British North America Act

8. What did the Constitutional Act create?

    a) Quebec and New Brunswick

    b) Ontario, Quebec, and Nova Scotia

    c) Upper Canada and New Brunswick

    d) Upper Canada and Lower Canada

9. In what year was the first representative assembly elected in Nova Scotia?

    a) 1833

    b) 1812

    c) 1758

    d) 1793

10. Who helped abolish slavery in Upper Canada in 1793?

    a) Sir John A. Macdonald

    b) The Duke of Wellington

    c) John Graves Simcoe

    d) Mary Ann Shad

11. When did British Parliament abolish slavery throughout the whole empire?

    a) 1833

    b) 1823

    c) 1791

    d) 1812

12. What was the name of the secret network that helped black slaves escape to British North America?

    a) The Freedom Passage

    b) The Underground Railroad

    c) The Railroad of Freedom

    d) The Tunnel to Canada

Review Questions – Chapter 4

1. Why did the British pass the Quebec Act of 1774?

2. What were the religious differences between the British and the French?

3. By what two names were the French–speaking Catholics of Quebec known?

4. Why did the Loyalists come to Canada during the American Revolution?

5. What year was the Constitutional Act passed?

6. What two things did the Constitutional Act do?

7. What were the British lands in North America called before 1867?

8. What did John Graves Simcoe help abolish in Upper Canada?

9. Where was slavery abolished in 1833?

10. What was the Underground Railroad?

Chapter 5

THE WAR OF 1812

At the beginning of the nineteenth century, France (led by the Emperor Napoleon) and the British Empire were fighting against each other. The United States of America thought that since the British had their hands full with the French, it would be a convenient time to invade and conquer British North America (Canada). In 1812, the Americans invaded the land that is now called Canada.

First Nation volunteers (including the famous Shawnee leader Chief Tecumseh) and Canadian volunteers helped British Soldiers defend British North America.

Here are some important battles and locations:

- 1812, Queenston Heights (near Niagara Falls) – Major–General Sir Isaac Brock successfully defended against the Americans.

- 1813, Chateauguay (near Montreal) – Lieutenant Colonel Charles de Sala-berry and 460 *Canadien* soldiers defeated 4,000 American soldiers.

- 1813, York (Toronto) – American invaders burned down the Parliament buildings.

- 1813, Boston Harbour – The British Ship HMS *Shannon* captured the American ship USS *Chesapeake*.

- 1813, Battle of Beaver Dams – A woman named Laura Secord travelled 30 km by foot to warn British Lieutenant James FitzGibbon that the Americans were planning an attack. The invading Americans were ambushed and captured.

- 1814, Washington – Major General Robert Ross and a British force went to Washington and burned down the White House.

Although the Americans won some battles, by 1814, their invasion was over. British North America was successfully defended. The border that still exists today between Canada and the United States is mainly a result of the end of the War of 1812.

After the War

Not all British North Americans were happy with the British monarchy and some even thought that British North America should join the United States. In 1837–1838, some of these reformers rebelled in Toronto and near Montreal. Since they were small in numbers, they were quickly defeated. Even though the Rebellions of 1837–1838 were small, they signified that some reform needed to happen in Canada.

A British reformer named Lord Durham wrote a report on the rebellions. Durham suggested that Upper Canada and Lower Canada should join together. Shortly after, in 1840, they joined together to form the **Province of Canada**.

Durham also recommended that the French *Canadiens* should learn to speak English. This idea was not appreciated by the *Canadiens* who celebrated their unique culture in British North America.

Durham's most important idea was that Canada needed a **responsible government**. This meant that the British governors in Canada would need the support of the elected members of the parliament. This marked one more step towards Canadian independence. This style of government still exists today in Canada.

In 1847–1848, Nova Scotia formed a responsible government. Shortly after, the Province of Canada (also called United Canada) formed a responsible government in 1848–1849 with the help of Governor Lord Elgin. **Finally, in 1849, Sir Louis–Hippolyte La Fontaine became the first leader of a responsible government in the Canadas**. This position is similar to what a Prime Minister is today. Robert Baldwin and Joseph Howe were other important reformers who helped make responsible governments possible.

Multiple-Choice Questions – Chapter 5

1. Who invaded British North America (Canada) in 1812?

   a) France

   b) The United States

   c) Spain

   d) Belgium

2. Who was Chief Tecumseh?

   a) An American military general

   b) A Canadian militiaman

   c) A famous Shawnee leader

   d) A Quebecois brigadier general

3. Who travelled 30 km by foot to warn the British that the Americans were planning an attack in 1813?

   a) Major–General Sir Isaac Brock

   b) The Duke of Wellington

   c) Lieutenant James Fitzgibbon

   d) Laura Secord

4. What did Major General Robert Ross and a British force burn down in 1814?

   a) The Parliament buildings

   b) Fort York

   c) Fort George

   d) The White House

5. What is the former name of Toronto?

    a) Bytown

    b) York

    c) Stadacona

    d) Hamilton

6. What happened in Toronto and near Montreal between 1837 and 1838?

    a) A flu epidemic

    b) An American invasion

    c) A great fire

    d) Rebellions

7. What happened to the Rebellions of 1837–1838?

    a) The rebels overthrew the government

    b) The rebels were defeated

    c) The rebels escaped to Europe

    d) The rebels captured the Parliament buildings

8. Who suggested that Upper Canada and Lower Canada be united in 1840?

    a) Lord Durham

    b) Robert Baldwin

    c) Sir George–Etienne Cartier

    d) Joseph Howe

9. What was the name of the new province that was formed by the joining of Upper and Lower Canada?

    a) Prince Rupert's Land

    b) The Province of Quebec

    c) The Province of Canada

    d) The Province of Ontario

10. What kind of government did Lord Durham recommend in Canada?

    a) Parliamentary democracy

    b) Responsible government

    c) A dictatorship

    d) Representational democracy

11. Who became the head of the first *responsible government* in Canada in 1849?

    a) Sir Louis–Hippolyte La Fontaine

    b) Sir John A. Macdonald

    c) Lord Durham

    d) Robert Baldwin

12. What position is this similar to in today's government?

    a) The Premier

    b) The Governor General

    c) The Prime Minister

    d) The Lieutenant Governor

Review Questions – Chapter 5

1. Why did the Americans think it would be easy to invade British North America in 1812?

2. What three groups successfully defended British North America from the American invaders?

3. What Major–General successfully defended Queenston Heights from the Americans in 1812?

4. Did the border between Canada and the United States change after the War of 1812?

5. Why did some British North Americans decide to lead rebellions in 1837–1838?

6. Were all French *Canadiens* happy with some of Lord Durham's recommendations? Why or why not?

7. What new province formed in 1840?

8. What does *responsible government* mean?

9. Who was Sir Louis–Hippolyte La Fontaine?

10. Who were two other important reformers that worked towards *responsible government?*

Chapter 6

THE CONFEDERATION OF CANADA

On **July 1, 1867,** the British Parliament passed **the British North America Act**, which made the Dominion of Canada a self–governing nation. The name *Dominion of Canada* was first mentioned by Sir Leonard Tilley, an official from New Brunswick. From then on, July 1 became a holiday called *Dominion Day*. Today, it is simply called *Canada Day*.

The groundwork of Confederation was developed by a group of men called the *Fathers of Confederation* that met between 1864 and 1867. Together, these men made many important decisions that would affect the future of Canada. They decided to make two levels of government: provincial and federal. They also decided that the Province of Canada would be broken up into two new provinces: Ontario and Quebec. A *Canadien* named George–Etienne Cartier helped bring Quebec into the Confederation. Alongside Cartier, Sir Etienne–Paschal was another popular Father of Confederation.

The first four provinces of Canada were Ontario, Quebec, New Brunswick, and Nova Scotia. Sir John A. Macdonald, an immigrant from Scotland, became the first Prime Minister of Canada.

Slowly, other provinces and territories started to join Canada:

Manitoba and Northwest Territories joined in 1870; British Columbia joined in 1871; Prince Edward Island joined in 1873; Yukon Territory joined in 1898; Alberta and Saskatchewan joined in 1905; Newfoundland and Labrador joined in 1949; and Nunavut joined in 1999.

Multiple-Choice Questions – Chapter 6

1. What act was passed on July 1, 1867?

   a) The Quebec Act

   b) The Constitutional Act

   c) The British North America Act

   d) The Confederation Act

2. Who first mentioned the *Dominion of Canada*?

   a) Joseph Howe

   b) Sir George–Etienne Cartier

   c) Sir Leonard Tilley

   d) Sir John A. Macdonald

3. What holiday do Canadians celebrate on July 1?

   a) Victoria Day

   b) Canada Day

   c) Independence Day

   d) Remembrance Day

4. What were the first four provinces of the Confederation?

   a) Ontario, New Brunswick, Nova Scotia, and P.E.I.

   b) Ontario, Quebec, Nova Scotia, and P.E.I.

   c) Quebec, Nova Scotia, Ontario, and New Brunswick

   d) Quebec, P.E.I., Nova Scotia, and New Brunswick

5. Who became the first Prime Minister of Canada?

    a) Louis Riel

    b) George–Etienne Cartier

    c) Leonard Tilley

    d) John A. Macdonald

6. What was the last province to join the Confederation of Canada?

    a) Manitoba

    b) Newfoundland and Labrador

    c) Nunavut

    d) British Columbia

Review Questions – Chapter 6

1. What happened on July 1, 1867?

2. What does the word *confederation* mean?

3. Who were the *Fathers of Confederation*?

4. Who helped bring Quebec into the Confederation?

5. What were the first four provinces to make up the Confederation?

6. What was the last territory to join the Confederation in 1999?

7. What year did Newfoundland and Labrador join the Confederation?

Chapter 7

LOUIS RIEL: THE FATHER OF MANITOBA

Louis Riel was a Metis politician, leader, and hero who wanted to protect the culture and heritage of the Metis people. Riel led a couple of rebellions in what would later become the Province of Manitoba. Riel is known as *the Father of Manitoba.*

1869, The Red River Rebellion – Louis Riel and a small army captured Fort Garry (now Winnipeg). Riel and the Metis were upset, because when the government of Canada acquired all of the land that the Hudson's Bay Company owned in 1869, they never thought to consult with the Metis people who lived on the land.

1870 – Riel left for the United States as the Canadian military retook Fort Garry. Shortly after, Manitoba joined Confederation. Riel was elected to Manitoba's new parliament even though he was living outside of the country.

1873 – Sir John A. Macdonald founded the North West Mounted Police (NWMP) to look after the new land that Canada was acquiring in the North West. The NWMP eventually became the Royal Canadian Mounted Police (RCMP), Canada's national police force. Sir Sam Steele, a famous Canadian soldier, began his career as a member of the North West Mounted Police.

1885, Northwest Rebellion – Metis and Aboriginal groups led another rebellion in what is now Alberta and Saskatchewan because they felt that their rights were in danger. The Metis' military was led by Gabriel Dumont. After five months, the Canadian military defeated the rebels and Louis Riel was executed for treason.

The Canadian Pacific Railway

British Columbia agreed to join the Confederation if the government built a railway to connect to the west coast. In **1885**, the Canadian Pacific Railway was completed. **The Railway symbolized Canadian unity**. Lord Strathcona (Donald Smith) drove in the last railway spike. Thousands of Chinese workers came to Canada to help build the railway.

THE HEAD TAX

After the railway was finished, many of the Chinese workers wanted to bring their families to Canada. The government of Canada started charging a Head Tax for each Chinese person entering Canada. This was a form of discrimination. In 2006, the government of Canada apologized for the Head Tax.

The Canadian Pacific Railway helped the country grow west of Ontario. Both the population and the economy grew. Millions of immigrants moved to Canada after the railway was finished. Many immigrants from Europe started to move west to farm.

Multiple-Choice Questions – Chapter 7

1. Who is the Father of Manitoba?

   a) Gabriel Dumont

   b) Sir John A. Macdonald

   c) Louis Riel

   d) Lord Strathcona

2. What aboriginal group did Louis Riel belong to?

   a) Metis

   b) Inuit

   c) First Nations

   d) Dene

3. What fort did Riel and his supporters seize in 1869?

   a) Fort York

   b) Fort Henry

   c) Fort George

   d) Fort Garry

4. What police force did Sir John A. Macdonald create in 1873?

   a) Royal Canadian Mounted Police

   b) North West Mounted Police

   c) Ontario Provincial Police

   d) Canadian Security Intelligence Service

5. Who was a great Metis military leader?

   a) Sir John A. Macdonald

   b) Sir Sam Steele

   c) Lord Strathcona

   d) Gabriel Dumont

6. What happened to Louis Riel?

   a) He was executed for treason

   b) He escaped to the United States

   c) He was killed during the Red River Rebellions

   d) He became the Premier of Manitoba

7. In what year was the Canadian Pacific Railway completed?

   a) 1875

   b) 1885

   c) 1867

   d) 1895

8. What province agreed to join Confederation if the railway was completed?

   a) British Columbia

   b) Saskatchewan

   c) Manitoba

   d) Alberta

9. What was the Canadian Pacific Railway a symbol of?

   a) Economic strength

   b) Canadian unity

   c) Peace

   d) The lumber industry

10. Who drove in the last spike in the Canadian Pacific Railway?

   a) Lord Strathcona

   b) Sir John A. Macdonald

   c) Sir Sanford Fleming

   d) Sir Arthur Currie

11. What immigrant group helped build the Canadian Pacific Railway?

    a) Polish
    b) Italian
    c) Irish
    d) Chinese

12. What discriminatory tax did many Chinese immigrants face after the railway was completed?

    a) The H.S.T.
    b) The Head Tax
    c) The Visa Tax
    d) The G.S.T.

Review Questions – Chapter 7

1. Who was Louis Riel?

2. Why were Louis Riel and other Metis upset with the Canadian government in 1869?

3. Who were the North West Mounted Police and who did they later become?

4. Who was Gabriel Dumont?

5. What was Louis Riel executed for?

6. What did British Columbia want built before it joined the Confederation?

7. What immigrant group helped build the Canadian Pacific Railway?

8. What did the government of Canada apologize for in 2006?

9. What did Lord Strathcona do?

10. What changes happened to Canada after the railway was completed?

Chapter 8

CANADA IN WORLD WAR I (1914–1918)

When the British Empire declared war on Germany in 1914, the Canadian Expeditionary Force was more than willing to help out. **Canada supplied over 600,000 soldiers in the First World War**. Over 3,000 Canadian nurses, called **Bluebirds**, helped in the war effort.

The Canadian military had international experience before World War I, since they had fought in the Boer War (South African War) of 1899–1900.

Key dates in World War I:

– April 9, 1917 – Battle of Vimy Ridge

Over 10,000 Canadians were killed or hurt when they took control of the ridge. After this battle, April 9 became known as Vimy Day.

– August 8, 1918 – Battle of Amiens

Canadian soldiers joined the British and French forces to defeat the Germans in a decisive victory. Canada's greatest soldier of World War I, General Sir Arthur Currie, became famous for his great command.

– November 11, 1918 – Armistice (Germany's surrender and the end of the war)

In the end 60,000 Canadian soldiers lost their lives and 170,000 were wounded. **November 11** became known as **Remembrance Day** in Canada. Canadians wear a red poppy and have a moment of silence at 11:00 a.m. to remember and honour all of the soldiers (110,000 in total) that have died defending Canada. Usually, Canadians recite a famous poem by **Colonel John McCrae** called **"In Flanders Fields."**

After World War I, the British Empire became the British Commonwealth (which now has fifty–three other nations). Canada is still part of the British Commonwealth.

A Changing Society

World War I brought change to Canada, both during the war and after.

In 1916, Manitoba became the first province to let women vote. Dr. Emily Stowe, who was the first female doctor in Canada, led the women's suffrage movement (*suffrage* means the right to vote).

Shortly after, in 1917, when Sir Robert Borden was the prime minister, nurses (the Bluebirds) and female relatives of soldiers were given the right to vote. **In 1918, female citizens of Canada were allowed to vote in federal elections.** Agnes Macphail became the first female MP in 1921. In 1940, Quebec allowed women to vote. This was due to the work of Therese Casgrain, who led the women's suffrage movement in Quebec.

After the stock market crash in 1929, Canada's economy, which had done well in the "Roaring Twenties," crashed and unemployment levels climbed to 27 percent. To help stabilize the economy, the Bank of Canada was created in 1934.

Multiple-Choice Questions – Chapter 8

1. How many soldiers did Canada supply in World War I?

    a) About 40,000

    b) More than 600,000

    c) 8 million

    d) 3,000

2. How many Canadian *Bluebird* nurses helped in World War I?

    a) About 5,000

    b) About 1,000

    c) More than 7,000

    d) More than 3,000

3. How many Canadian soldiers were killed or injured during the Battle of Vimy Ridge?

    a) 10,000

    b) 1,000

    c) 100,000

    d) 50,000

4. When is Vimy Day?

    a) March 3

    b) November 11

    c) April 9

    d) May 24

5. Who was Canada's greatest soldier in World War I?

    a) Sir Arthur Currie

    b) Sir Sam Steele

    c) Phil Edwards

    d) John McCrae

6. When is Remembrance Day observed?

    a) June 24

    b) January 11

    c) April 9

    d) November 11

7. What do Canadians wear on Remembrance Day?

    a) A white lily

    b) A red poppy

    c) A red rose

    d) A red maple leaf

8. Who wrote "In Flanders Fields"?

    a) Arthur Currie

    b) Rohinton Mistry

    c) Margaret Atwood

    d) John McCrae

9. How many Canadian soldiers died in World War I?

    a) 80,000

    b) 600,000

    c) 60,000

    d) 40,000

10. What Canadian province became the first to let women vote?

    a) Ontario

    b) Manitoba

    c) British Columbia

    d) Quebec

11. Who led the women's suffrage movement in Canada?

    a) Dr. Emily Stowe

    b) Agnes Macphail

    c) Kim Campbell

    d) Adrienne Clarkson

12. Who became Canada's first female MP?

    a) Roberta Borden

    b) Lucy Maud Montgomery

    c) Dr. Emily Stowe

    d) Agnes Macphail

Review Questions – Chapter 8

1. What took place between 1914 and 1918?

2. In what other war did Canadians help fight in at the beginning of the twentieth century?

3. When was the Battle of Amiens?

4. What happened on November 11, 1918?

5. After World War I, what did the British Empire become?

6. Who was Dr. Emily Stowe?

7. Who was Agnes Macphail?

8. When were women allowed to vote in Quebec?

9. What happened in 1929?

10. When was the bank of Canada created?

Chapter 9

CANADA IN WORLD WAR II
(1939–1945)

In 1939, Canada joined Britain and France in the war against Adolf Hitler and Nazi Germany. Over one million soldiers from Canada and Newfoundland (Newfoundland didn't join Confederation until 1949) fought in World War II.

Canada's RCAF (Royal Canadian Air Force) became important in the war, and Canada even supplied training to 130,000 Allied aircrew. The Royal Canadian Navy also became an important factor in defending against German U–boats (submarines).

KEY BATTLES AND DATES:

1941 – The Defence of Hong Kong

- Canadian soldiers lost Hong Kong to the invading Japanese army.

1942 – Dieppe Raid

- Canadian soldiers tried to take control of Dieppe on the northern coast of France and were forced to retreat.

June 6, 1944 – The D–Day Invasion

  – Canadian soldiers (15,000 strong) successfully attacked the German army at
    Juno Beach in Normandy in France. The Canadian army went on to free the
    Netherlands from Nazi Germany.

May 8, 1945 – Germany surrendered

August 14, 1945 – Japan surrendered

By the end of World War II, 44,000 Canadian soldiers had lost their lives.

While most fighting took place in Europe or Asia, the only attack on Canadian soil
took place on Vancouver Island, where Japan attacked a lighthouse with a submarine. Japan also sent balloon bombs over the western provinces of Canada.

Since Japan was an enemy of Canada during the war, the government of Canada
unfortunately decided to detain Japanese Canadians. The government also seized
their property. In 1988, the government of Canada apologized for its wrongdoing.

Multiple Choice Questions – Chapter 9

1. When did Canada join World War II?

    a) 1935

    b) 1939

    c) 1918

    d) 1945

2. How many Canadians and Newfoundlanders served in World War II?

    a) About 10,000

    b) About 100,000

    c) More than 1 million

    d) About half a million

3. When was D–Day?

    a) September 3, 1945

    b) November 11, 1944

    c) November 11, 1945

    d) June 6, 1944

4. When did Germany surrender?

    a) May 8, 1945

    b) November 11, 1945

    c) June 6, 1945

    d) June 6, 1944

5. How many Canadian soldiers were killed in World War II?

    a) 33,000

    b) 400,000

    c) 44,000

    d) 80,000

6. When did the government of Canada apologize to Japanese Canadians for the mistreatment they endured during World War II?

    a) 2006

    b) 1996

    c) 2008

    d) 1988

Review Questions – Chapter 9

1. What countries were Canada and its Allies fighting against in World War II?

2. What is the RCAF and why was it important in World War II?

3. What were two battles that Canadian soldiers lost?

4. What happened during the D–Day Invasion?

5. Describe the only attack that happened on Canadian soil.

6. What happened to Canadians of Japanese origin during World War II?

Chapter 10

CANADA IN THE MODERN WORLD

A fter World War II, the quality of life in Canada improved along with the economy. This was due to several reasons.

Economic reasons:

- The General Agreement on Tariffs and Trade (now the World Trade Organization) was signed and helped Canada trade with other countries.

- Oil was discovered in Alberta in 1947.

- Between 1945–1970, Canada's economy was one of the strongest in the world and Canada's trading relationship with the United States grew stronger.

Social Assistance Programs:

- The Canada Health Act provided basic health care to everyone.

- In 1940 Employment Insurance was instituted.

- In 1927 the Old Age Security was planned.

- In 1965 the Canada and Quebec Pension Plans were started.

Canada's Alliances

Canada joined other countries in NATO (North Atlantic Treaty Organization) and also formed NORAD with the US to form military alliances against the Soviet Union in the Cold War.

Canada also joined the United Nations (UN) and was part of the UN effort in the Korean War, which led to 500 Canadian soldier casualties. Canadian soldiers are famous for helping in UN peacekeeping missions. Canada has helped in Afghanistan, the former Yugoslavia, Egypt, Cyprus and Haiti.

New Immigrants

In 1956, 37,000 Hungarians came to Canada to escape Communism. After the Vietnam War broke out in 1975, over 50,000 Vietnamese refugees came to Canada.

The Right to Vote

In 1948 Japanese–Canadians were given the right to vote. Aboriginal people were given the right to vote in 1960.

The Quiet Revolution in Quebec

After World War II, Quebec prospered due to many changes and new laws. The changes that happened in Quebec in the 1960s are called **the Quiet Revolution**.

The following changes helped transform Quebec:

- The Royal Commission on Bilingualism and Biculturalism was introduced in 1963.

- In 1969, **the Official Languages Act** was passed. This meant that English or French would be offered for all federal services, and it would also maintain equality between French and English in Canada.

- *La Francophonie* (an association) was founded in 1970 between Canada and other Francophone countries.

THE POPULARITY OF QUEBEC SOVEREIGNTY

In 1980 and 1995, Quebec held two referendums to vote on whether or not they should separate from Canada. Both times the idea of sovereignty (independence) lost.

Multiple-Choice Questions – Chapter 10

1. What valuable resource was discovered in Alberta in 1947?

    a) Dinosaur fossils

    b) Oil

    c) Gold

    d) Uranium

2. What year was Employment Insurance introduced?

    a) 1950

    b) 1949

    c) 1940

    d) 1969

3. When was the Canadian Pension Plan introduced?

    a) 1965

    b) 1940

    c) 1939

    d) 1945

4. What organizations has Canada joined?

    a) NATO

    b) NORAD

    c) UN

    d) All of the above

5. How many Canadians died in the Korean War?

    a) 300

    b) 100

    c) 1,000

    d) 500

6. When were Aboriginal people granted the right to vote?

    a) 1945

    b) 1970

    c) 1948

    d) 1960

7. What were the changes that happened in Quebec during the 1960s known as?

    a) The Noise Movement

    b) The Calm Storm

    c) The Silent Rebellion

    d) The Quiet Revolution

8. What act declared that English and French would be offered for all federal services?

    a) The Constitution Act

    b) The Official Languages Act

    c) The Official Bilingual Act

    d) The Quebec Act

9. When was *La Francophonie* founded?

    a) 1975

    b) 1965

    c) 1960

    d) 1970

10. In which two years did Quebec hold a referendum?

    a) 1980 and 1985

    b) 1983 and 1985

    c) 1980 and 1995

    d) 1990 and 1995

Review Questions – Chapter 10

1. What factors contributed to Canada's growth after World War II?

2. What social assistance programs were introduced during or after World War II?

3. What alliances did Canada form or join after World War II?

4. In what countries have Canadian UN peacekeepers helped?

5. When were Japanese Canadians granted the right to vote?

6. What was *the Quiet Revolution*?

7. What was the Official Languages Act of 1969?

8. Why did Quebec hold two referendums in 1980 and 1995?

9. What was the outcome of each referendum?

Chapter 11

THE ARTS IN CANADA

Canada has a long history of famous visual artists, writers, poets, filmmakers, and musicians.

Famous writers and scholars: Robertson Davies, Pauline Johnson, Emile Nelligan, Marshall McLuhan, Harold Innis, Stephen Leacock, Margaret Laurence, Louis Hemon, Sir Charles G.D. Roberts, Mordecai Richler, Michael Ondaatje, Joy Kagawa, and Rohinton Mistry.

Famous musicians: Healey Willan, Sir Ernest MacMillan, and jazz pianist Oscar Peterson.

Famous visual artists: The Group of Seven. (This group of seven artists was founded in 1920 and painted natural landscapes. Emily Carr, an artist that became famous for painting Aboriginal totem poles on the West Coast of Canada became close friends of the Group of Seven.)

- Les Automatistes were a group of abstract painters from Quebec. Jean–Paul Riopelle was a part of this group.
- Louis–Phillippe Hebert is a famous sculptor.
- Kenojuak Ashevak is a famous Inuit artist.
- Bill Reid is a famous Haida artist. Reid is famous for his sculptures and totem poles.

Famous filmmakers: Denys Arcand, Norman Jewison, and Atom Egoyan.

Canadian Sports and Athletes

Hockey is Canada's official winter sport, and it is also the most popular sport in Canada. Teams in the National Hockey League (NHL) try to win the Stanley Cup, which was donated by former Governor General Lord Stanley. Women's hockey teams try to win the Clarkson Cup, which was started by Governor General Adrienne Clarkson in 2005.

The Canadian Football League (CFL) is also very popular in Canada. Teams try to win the Grey Cup, which was given in 1909 by the Governor General of Canada, Lord Grey.

Lacrosse is Canada's official summer sport.

Some other highlights from the history of sports in Canada:

In 1891, James Naismith invented basketball.

Marjorie Turner–Bailey was an Olympian whose family was originally black Loyalists.

Phil Edwards was a doctor, soldier, and Olympian who won bronze medals for Canada in track and field.

In 1996, Donovan Bailey won two gold medals in sprinting at the Olympics.

Chantal Petitclerc has won gold medals at several Paralympic Games in wheelchair racing.

In 1972, Canada won Olympic–hockey gold against the Soviet Union at the Olympics. Paul Henderson scored the winning goal.

Terry Fox started to run across Canada in 1980. Fox lost one leg to cancer and his *Marathon of Hope* raised money for Cancer Research. Even though Fox passed away before he could finish his run, his *Marathon of Hope* still lives on today.

Rick Hansen travelled around the world in his wheelchair to raise money for medical research.

Mark Tewkesbury is a famous Olympic Gold medalist in swimming and Catrina Le May Doan is a famous speed skater who won gold at the 2002 Olympics.

Multiple-Choice Questions – Chapter 11

1. Who are two famous Canadian writers?

    a) Robertson Davies and Oscar Peterson

    b) Robertson Davies and Healey Willan

    c) Margaret Laurence and Mordecai Richler

    d) Margaret Laurence and Emily Carr

2. Who is a famous Canadian musician?

    a) Pauline Johnson

    b) Robertson Davies

    c) Joy Kagawa

    d) Oscar Peterson

3. Who was the *Group of Seven*?

    a) A group of landscape painters

    b) A group of poets

    c) A Canadian jazz band

    d) A group of Inuit sculptors

4. Who is a famous Inuit artist?

    a) Kenojuak Ashevak

    b) Denys Arcand

    c) Jean–Paul Riopelle

    d) Emily Carr

5. Who is Atom Egoyan?

   a) A writer

   b) A painter

   c) A filmmaker

   d) A sculptor

6. Who is famous for painting totem poles on the West Coast of Canada?

   a) Jean–Paul Riopelle

   b) Emily Carr

   c) Denys Arcand

   d) Robertson Davies

7. What is Canada's official winter sport?

   a) Lacrosse

   b) Basketball

   c) Hockey

   d) Football

8. What do teams in the CFL try to win?

   a) The Clarkson Cup

   b) The Stanley Cup

   c) The Grey Cup

   d) The Ryder Cup

9. Who invented basketball in 1891?

   a) James Naismith

   b) Lord Grey

   c) Mark Tewksbury

   d) Terry Fox

10. Who started *the Marathon of Hope* in 1980?

   a) Donovan Bailey

   b) Terry Fox

   c) Catriona Le May Doan

   d) James Naismith

11. Who scored the winning goal in the famous 1972 hockey game against the Soviet Union at the Olympics?

   a) Paul Henderson

   b) Wayne Gretzky

   c) Sidney Crosby

   d) Donovan Bailey

12. What is Canada's official summer sport?

   a) Football

   b) Baseball

   c) Hockey

   d) Lacrosse

Review Questions – Chapter 11

1. Who are three famous Canadian writers or scholars?

2. Who are three famous Canadian artists?

3. What kind of art did *the Group of Seven* paint?

4. Who is a famous Canadian filmmaker?

5. What are Canada's two official sports?

6. What sport do they play in the CFL?

7. Who is a famous Canadian sprinter?

8. Who is Terry Fox and what did he do?

9. How did Rick Hansen travel around the world?

10. Who is a famous Canadian speed skater?

Chapter 12

SCIENCE AND TECHNOLOGY

IN CANADA

Canadian technology and science is known all over the world. The Canadian Space Agency and astronauts have been active in space exploration since 1989. A huge mechanical arm called *the Canadarm* was used by NASA for thirty years. *The Canadarm* was invented by SPAR Aerospace and the National Research Council. Canada also has many Nobel Prize winners: Gerhard Herzberg, John Polanyi, Richard E. Taylor, Bertram Brockhouse, Michael Smith, and Sidney Altman.

FAMOUS INVENTIONS AND DISCOVERIES BY CANADIANS

Sir Frederick Banting and Charles Best discovered insulin. This discovery helped diabetes patients all around the world.

- Alexander Graham Bell developed the telephone.
- Joseph–Armand Bombardier invented the snowmobile.
- Reginald Fessenden helped invent the radio.
- Sir Sanford Fleming invented the Standard Time Zone system.
- Matthew Evans and Henry Woodward invented the electric light bulb.
- Dr. Wilder Penfield was a famous brain surgeon.
- Dr. John A. Hopps invented the pacemaker.
- Mike Laziridis and Jim Balsillie started RIM (Research In Motion) and invented its famous phone the Blackberry.

Multiple-Choice Questions – Chapter 12

1. What huge mechanical arm invented by SPAR was used by NASA for thirty years?

    a) The Manitobarm

    b) The Canadarm

    c) The Canadian Elbow

    d) The Hubble telescope

2. Who is a Canadian Nobel Prize winner?

    a) Sir Sanford Fleming

    b) Robertson Davies

    c) Louis–Phillippe Hebert

    d) John Polanyi

3. Who discovered insulin?

    a) Sir Frederick Banting and Matthew Evans

    b) Alexander Graham Bell

    c) Matthew Evans and Henry Woodward

    d) Sir Frederick Banting and Charles Best

4. What did Alexander Graham Bell develop?

    a) The radio

    b) The pacemaker

    c) The telephone

    d) The snowmobile

5. Who developed the Standard Time Zone system?

    a) Sir Sanford Fleming

    b) Joseph–Armand Bombardier

    c) Matthew Evans and Henry Woodward

    d) Charles Best

6. What product is RIM famous for?

    a) The Blueberry

    b) The smartphone

    c) The pager

    d) The Blackberry

Review Questions – Chapter 12

1. Who invented the Canadarm?

2. Who are three Canadian Nobel Prize winners?

3. Why was the discovery of insulin by Sir Frederick Banting and Charles Best so important?

4. Who invented the snowmobile?

5. Who is a famous Canadian brain surgeon?

6. Who invented the pacemaker?

7. Who helped invent the radio?

Chapter 13

THE CANADIAN GOVERNMENT

There are three important facts about the Canadian government. The Canadian government is a **federal state**, a **parliamentary democracy**, and a **constitutional monarchy**.

FEDERAL STATE

Canada has different levels of government: federal, provincial, territorial, and municipal. In a **federal state**, different levels of government can sometimes work together but at other times work independently. The federal and provincial governments have their own responsibilities, but they also share some responsibilities as well.

Some federal responsibilities include defence, foreign policy, currency, criminal law, citizenship, trade between provinces, and aboriginal affairs.

Some provincial responsibilities include education, health care, highways, civil rights, and municipal governments.

Some shared responsibilities (both federal and provincial) include immigration, agriculture, and environment.

PARLIAMENTARY DEMOCRACY

Parliamentary democracy means that Canada's elected government meets in Ottawa at the House of Commons.

Parliament has three parts: **the House of Commons, the Senate, and the Sovereign (King or Queen).**

CONSTITUTIONAL MONARCHY

Constitutional monarchy means that the **Head of State** in Canada is the Sovereign (Queen or King).

In Canada, the **head of state** is the King or Queen of England (currently Elizabeth II) and the **head of government** is the Prime Minister.

The Sovereign (Queen Elizabeth) is represented by the Governor General in Canada. The Governor General is chosen by the Sovereign (with advice from the Prime Minister) about every five years.

In a province, a **Lieutenant Governor** represents the Sovereign. A Lieutenant Governor is chosen by the Governor General (with advice from the Prime Minister) to represent the Sovereign in each of the provinces about every five years.

Multiple-Choice Questions – Chapter 13

1. What is an important fact about the Canadian government?

    a) It is a constitutional monarchy

    b) It is a federal state

    c) It is a parliamentary democracy

    d) All of the above

2. What level of government is responsible for *citizenship*?

    a) The municipal level

    b) The federal level

    c) The provincial level

    d) All of the above

3. What are the three parts of Parliament?

    a) The Senate, the Sovereign, and the Prime Minister

    b) The House of Commons, the Lieutenant Governor, and the Senate

    c) The House of Commons, the Senate, and the Sovereign

    d) The Prime Minister, the Senate, and the Sovereign

4. Who is the *head of state* in Canada?

    a) The president

    b) The Prime Minister

    c) The Queen or King of England

    d) The Governor General

5. Who represents the Sovereign in Canada?

    a) The Governor General

    b) The Lieutenant General

    c) The Prime Minister

    d) The Senate

6. Who represents the Sovereign in the provinces?

    a) A Senator

    b) A Lieutenant Governor

    c) A Commissioner

    d) A Member of Parliament

Review Questions – Chapter 13

1. What are three important facts about the government of Canada?

2. What are some shared responsibilities between the federal and provincial governments?

3. Who is the *head of state* in Canada?

4. Who is the *head of government* in Canada?

5. Who does the Governor General represent in Canada?

6. How is the Governor General chosen?

7. What is a Lieutenant Governor?

Chapter 14

THE THREE LEVELS OF GOVERNMENT

Canada has three levels of government: **federal**, **provincial** (or territorial), and **municipal** (city).

THE FEDERAL GOVERNMENT

The federal government meets in the Parliament buildings in Ottawa. The **Prime Minister** is the head of the federal government and elected **members of Parliament** (MPs) represent the people of Canada.

THE PROVINCIAL AND TERRITORIAL GOVERNMENTS

A Premier is the head of a provincial government. In the territories, a Commissioner represents the federal government.

Provincial governments meet at a **Legislative Assembly** in their capital cities.

Each province and territory has elected representatives that work in their provincial or territorial legislative assembly. Each province or territory calls these elected representatives by a different name. They are called either MPPs (members of Provincial Parliament), MNAs (members of the National Assembly), MLAs (members of the Legislative Assembly), or MHAs (Members of the House of Assembly).

The Municipal Government

Cities have a municipal government (or local government). Municipal governments take care of local responsibilities. City councillors are elected by the city's residents and sit at a council. A mayor (or sometimes reeve) is the head of the municipal government. Together, the city council passes city laws called by-laws. By-laws are different from city to city.

Some examples of municipal responsibilities include urban planning, snow removal, police services, and firefighting.

First Nations who live on reserves have a different system of government. Reserves have councillors and band chiefs who make decisions about reserve services such as housing and schools.

The Three Branches of Government

There are three branches of government in Canada: **the Executive**, **the Legislative**, and **the Judicial**.

The executive branch makes or executes decisions. The Cabinet (including the Prime Minister) and the Sovereign (and the Governor General) are part of this.

The legislative branch makes laws. It is made up of the House of Commons, the Senate, and the Queen (and the Governor General).

The judicial branch includes Canada's courts and judges. The Supreme Court of Canada has nine judges who are chosen by the Governor General.

MAKING LAWS IN CANADA

Before a law is official, it is called a **bill**. For a bill to become a law, it must follow certain steps. First, it is read in the House of Commons. Then it is read again. Next, a committee reviews the bill. Then members of Parliament have an option to make changes (called amendments) to it. Then it is read a third time, and then MPs vote on it. If it is voted through, it then passes to the Senate. Finally, if the senators agree, the bill receives **Royal Assent**, is signed by the Governor General, and becomes an official law.

Multiple-Choice Questions – Chapter 14

1. What are the three levels of government?

    a) Federal, provincial, and state

    b) Federal, electoral district, and municipality

    c) Federal, parliamentary, and municipal

    d) Federal, provincial (or territorial), and municipal

2. Where does the federal government meet?

    a) In the Parliament buildings in Ottawa

    b) At Queen's Park in Toronto

    c) In Ottawa's city hall

    d) In the Parliament buildings in Toronto

3. Who is the head of the federal government?

    a) The Queen

    b) The Prime Minister

    c) The Governor General

    d) The minister of Finance

4. Who is the head of a provincial government?

    a) The Prime Minister

    b) A mayor

    c) A Premier

    d) A commissioner

5. What are the three branches of government?

    a) The executive, the legislative, and the judicial

    b) The executive, the legislative, and the parliamentary

    c) The legislative, the judicial, and the disciplinary

    d) The executive, the police force, and the judicial

6. What is a *law* called before it is official?

    a) A bill

    b) A pre–law

    c) An amendment

    d) A legislature

Review Questions – Chapter 14

1. What are the three levels of government in Canada?

2. What are the three branches of government in Canada?

3. Who is the head of a municipal government?

4. What government branch is responsible for making laws?

5. Where do provincial governments meet?

6. What is an MP and who do they represent?

7. What is a by–law?

8. How many judges are there in the Supreme Court of Canada?

9. Describe the steps in which a bill becomes a law.

10. What does it mean when a bill has been given *Royal Assent*?

Chapter 15

ELECTIONS IN CANADA

Federal elections are held every four years, on the third Monday in October. Canadians who are **eighteen years or older**, **Canadian citizens**, and on the **voter's list** can vote for the candidate that they want to represent them in the House of Commons in Ottawa. Canadians who are on the voter's list receive a voter's information card in the mail that has the **polling station's** (the place where they will vote) location on it.

Canadian elections are by **secret ballot**. A ballot is a piece of paper that you vote on. No one has the right to know or to ask who you voted for unless you feel comfortable talking about it. Voters mark an "X" on the **ballot** beside the name of the candidate they want to vote for. If they are not able to go to vote on voting day, they can vote in an advance poll. Advance poll locations are also on the voter information card.

If a candidate wins the election, he or she will become that electoral district's **member of Parliament**. An electoral district (sometimes called a riding) is a bordered area that is represented by one member of Parliament. **There are 338 electoral districts in Canada.** This means that there are 338 **seats** in the House of Commons where MPs sit and represent their electoral district. Usually one electoral district will have many candidates running in the election.

Candidates in federal elections can be part of a political party or they can be independent. Currently, the largest political parties in Canada are the Conservatives, the Liberals, and the New Democratic Party (NDP).

How Do You Win an Election?

Whichever political party wins the most seats in a federal election will form the next government. The leader of the party that wins will become the Prime Minister. It is tradition that after an election the Governor General invites the political party with the most seats to become the next government.

The Prime Minister then chooses members of his party to become **Cabinet ministers.** Cabinet ministers operate government departments (i.e., defence, health, agriculture) and together they form what is called **the Cabinet**.

If the political party that wins has more than half of the seats in the House of Commons, then they will have a *majority government*. If they have less than half of the seats, they will have a *minority government*.

The party that has the second largest number of seats or members of Parliament after an election becomes the **Official Opposition** (also called **Her Majesty's Loyal Opposition**).

To remain in power, the government (the Prime Minister and their party) needs the *confidence* of at least 50 percent of the MPs in the House of Commons. If they don't have this *confidence* (determined by a vote), then an election can be called by the Governor General.

Multiple-Choice Questions – Chapter 15

1. Federal elections are held on the third Monday in which month?

    a) October
    b) November
    c) September
    d) December

2. What is a *polling station*?

    a) A place where candidates can register for the election
    b) A place where you vote
    c) A place where MPs work
    d) A place where political debates are held

3. What is the piece of paper you vote on called?

    a) A voter's list
    b) A riding
    c) An electoral district
    d) A ballot

4. How many electoral districts are there in Canada?

    a) 338
    b) 238
    c) 408
    d) 13

5. What do you call the group of politicians that control government departments?

    a) The Prime Minister

    b) The Governor General

    c) The Senate

    d) The Cabinet

6. What do you call the political party with the second largest number of seats in the federal government?

    a) A minority government

    b) A majority government

    c) Her Majesty's Loyal Opposition

    d) The official senate

Review Questions – Chapter 15

1. What three requirements do you need to meet in order to vote in a federal election?

2. How often are federal elections held?

3. What does *secret ballot* mean?

4. Who represents an electoral district?

5. How many seats are in the House of Commons?

6. What are the largest political parties in Canada?

7. How is it decided which political party forms the next government?

8. What does a *majority* government mean?

GOVERNMENT WORKSHEETS

My Federal Government

The Prime Minister of Canada is:

The Prime Minister's political party is:

The Governor General is:

The Official Opposition party is:

The Official Opposition leader is:

My member of Parliament is:

My MP's political party is:

My Provincial Government

The Premier of my province is:

The Premier's political party is:

The Lieutenant Governor's name is:

The Official Opposition party is:

My MPP's (or MLA's, MHA's, or MNA's) name is:

My MPP's (or MLA's, MHA's, or MNA's) political party is:

My Municipal Government

The mayor (or reeve) of my city is:

My councillor's name is:

Chapter 16

THE JUSTICE SYSTEM IN CANADA

In Canada, everyone is innocent until they are proven guilty. This is called *the presumption of innocence*. The government must treat all citizens fairly and respect their legal rights through the legal system. This is called *due process*.

COURTS IN CANADA

There are different levels of courts in Canada. The top court is the Supreme Court of Canada. The federal courts deal with national problems. There are also provincial courts, family courts, and small claims courts. **The courts' role is to settle disagreements or conflicts.**

POLICE IN CANADA

There are different types of police in Canada. **The police's job is to enforce the laws of Canada.** The Royal Canadian Mounted Police (RCMP) are the federal police. The RCMP are also the provincial police in all provinces except Ontario and Quebec. Ontario and Quebec have their own provincial police. Most cities have their own police force as well.

Multiple-Choice Questions – Chapter 16

1. Which of the following statements is correct?

    a) In Canada, everyone is innocent until proven guilty

    b) In Canada, everyone is guilty until proven innocent

    c) In Canada, you do not have the right to a fair trial

    d) All of the above

2. What is the top court of Canada?

    a) Provincial Court

    b) Family Court

    c) The Supreme Court

    d) Small Claims Court

3. Whose role is it to settle disagreements or conflicts?

    a) The municipality's

    b) The government's

    c) The police force's

    d) The court's

4. Whose job is it to enforce the laws of Canada?

    a) The courts'

    b) The police force's

    c) The MP's

    d) The judge's

5. Who are the federal police in Canada?

   a) The OPP

   b) The NWMP

   c) The RCMP

   d) CSIS

6. Which two provinces have their own provincial police?

   a) Ontario and British Columbia

   b) Quebec and Manitoba

   c) Alberta and Manitoba

   d) Ontario and Quebec

Review Questions – Chapter 16

1. What does the presumption of innocence mean?

2. What does due process mean?

3. What are different types of courts in Canada?

4. What is the role of the courts in Canada?

5. What is the role of the police in Canada?

6. Who are the RCMP?

7. Do most cities have their own police force?

8. Does Ontario have its own provincial police force?

Chapter 17

SYMBOLS OF CANADA

Canada has many famous symbols that are important to its heritage.

THE BEAVER

The beaver has been a symbol of Canada for a very long time. (It was even the symbol of the Hudson's Bay Company). Many groups and associations in Canada use the beaver as their symbol, including the Jean Baptiste Society, which started using the beaver as its symbol in 1834. It is also on the coat of arms of some provinces and cities. The beaver is the national animal of Canada.

THE MAPLE LEAF

The maple leaf is probably Canada's most famous symbol because it is on its national flag. Early French *Canadiens* used the maple leaf as a symbol, and it has also been used on uniforms and on grave markers for Canadian soldiers.

THE CANADIAN CROWN

The Crown is a symbol of Canada and its government. The Crown symbolizes the historical connection between Canada and the United Kingdom. Queen Elizabeth II has been Queen of Canada since 1952.

THE FLEUR–DE–LYS

The French word *fleur–de–lys* means "lily flower" in English. The lily has been a symbol of France for hundreds of years, and when French settlers came to Canada they continued to use the *fleur–de–lys* as a symbol. Today, the *fleur–de–lys* is on the flag of Quebec.

PARLIAMENT

The Parliament buildings in Ottawa were built using Gothic Revival architecture and were finished in the 1860s. French, English, and Aboriginal influences were also used in designing the many different parts of the buildings.

In 1916, there was a fire that destroyed the Centre Block of the Parliament buildings (a couple of years later it was rebuilt). Luckily, the library survived the fire.

At the top of the Peace Tower (which was built to commemorate World War I) there is a special room called the Memorial Chamber. In this room, the names of soldiers who have died for Canada are written down in *Books of Remembrance.*

CANADA'S MOTTO

"*A mari usque ad mare,*" is Canada's motto and is Latin for "From Sea to Sea." The motto is included on Canada's coat of arms.

THE FLAGS OF CANADA

Canada's current red and white flag was adopted in **1965** and is Canada's official national flag. The Union Jack is Canada's official royal flag. Before the maple leaf flag, the Red Ensign was used by the Canadian government.

Multiple-Choice Questions – Chapter 17

1. What is the national animal of Canada?

    a) The caribou

    b) The beaver

    c) The moose

    d) The polar bear

2. What is on Canada's national flag?

    a) A maple tree

    b) A beaver

    c) A pine cone

    d) A maple leaf

3. What symbol is on the flag of Quebec?

    a) A caribou

    b) A maple leaf

    c) A fleur–de–lys

    d) A rose

4. What was built at Parliament to commemorate World War I?

    a) The Senate

    b) The Centre Block

    c) The library

    d) The Peace Tower

5. What does Canada's motto mean?

    a) From sea to sea

    b) From the river to the sea

    c) Out of many, one

    d) The true north, strong and free

6. When was Canada's red and white maple leaf flag adopted as its official national flag?

    a) 1980

    b) 1916

    c) 1955

    d) 1965

Review Questions – Chapter 17

1. What are three famous Canadian symbols?

2. What does *fleur–de–lys* mean in English?

3. What happened to the Parliament buildings in 1916?

4. What is in the Memorial Chamber at the top of the Peace Tower?

5. What is Canada's motto?

6. What is Canada's official royal flag?

7. What flag did the Canadian government use before 1965?

Chapter 18

THE ECONOMY OF CANADA

Trading is an important part of Canada's economy. Canada has been practicing free trade with its biggest trading partner, the United States, since 1994. About 75 percent of Canada's exports (which accounts for billions of dollars) go to the United States.

In 1984, the North American Free Trade Agreement (NAFTA) was signed between Canada, the United States, and Mexico. Canada has one of the world's largest economies (top 10), and is part of the G8 (Canada, the United States, Japan, Italy, the United Kingdom, France, Russia, and Germany).

There are three main types of industry in Canada:

Service, Manufacturing, and Natural Resources

The service industries include jobs in communication, health care, education, and other jobs that help or serve people. This is the most popular job industry in Canada. More than 75 percent of Canadians work in the service industry.

The manufacturing industries include all jobs that produce or manufacture products to sell. Paper, technology, food, and automobiles are examples of products that are made in Canada.

The natural resource industries include agriculture, fishing, mining, energy, and forestry. Canada is fortunate to have many natural resources. A large part of Canadian exports are products from the natural resource industry.

Multiple-Choice Questions – Chapter 18

1. Who is Canada's biggest trading partner?

    a) England
    b) Japan
    c) The United States
    d) China

2. What three countries signed the North American Free Trade Agreement in 1984?

    a) Canada, the United States, and England
    b) Canada, the United States, and Mexico
    c) Canada, the United States, and China
    d) Canada, England, and France

3. What are the three main types of industry in Canada?

    a) Natural resources, computer technology, and automotive
    b) Service, communications, and hydroelectricity
    c) Natural resources, service, and communications
    d) Service, manufacturing, and natural resources

4. What is the most popular job industry in Canada?

    a) Natural resources
    b) Manufacturing
    c) Service
    d) Computers

5. Is Canada part of the G8?

    a) Yes

    b) No

    c) Sometimes

    d) Not anymore

6. Fishing, mining, and forestry are examples of what industry?

    a) Hydroelectric

    b) Natural resources

    c) Manufacturing

    d) Service

Review Questions – Chapter 18

1. What percentage of Canada's exports goes to the United States?

2. What trade agreement did Canada, the United States, and Mexico sign in 1984?

3. What are the three main types of industry in Canada?

4. What jobs are included in the service industry?

5. What jobs are included in the manufacturing industry?

6. What jobs are included in the natural resource industry?

Chapter 19

THE GEOGRAPHY OF CANADA

Here are some key facts about the geography of Canada:

Canada has three oceans surrounding it: **the Atlantic Ocean, the Pacific Ocean, and the Arctic Ocean**.

The **Canadian Shield** is an ancient crust of rock that lies underneath almost half of Canada and is important for the mining and forestry industry.

Canada has a population of about **thirty–five million people**.

Canada is the second largest country in the world (ten million sq. km).

Canada shares a long border with United States. It is the longest undefended border in the world.

Ottawa is the national capital of Canada. Ottawa was founded in 1857 by Queen Victoria. The original name for Ottawa was Bytown.

Canada has **ten provinces** and **three territories**.

The Five Regions of Canada

There are five regions in Canada: **the Atlantic Provinces, Central Canada, the Prairie Provinces, the West Coast, and the Northern Territories**.

1. THE ATLANTIC PROVINCES

(Newfoundland and Labrador, Prince Edward Island, Nova Scotia, and New Brunswick)

The Atlantic Provinces are on the east coast of Canada and their many natural resources (fishing, mining, etc.) are important to their economies.

2. CENTRAL CANADA

(Ontario and Quebec)

The population surrounding the Great Lakes and the Saint Lawrence River makes up more than 50 percent of Canada's total population. Seventy–five percent of all Canadian products are made in Central Canada, which is also known as "the manufacturing and industrial heartland."

3. THE PRAIRIE PROVINCES

(Alberta, Saskatchewan, and Manitoba)

The Prairie Provinces are famous for their farmland and for their energy resources.

4. THE WEST COAST

(British Columbia)

Bordering the Pacific Ocean, British Columbia has some of the most famous scenery in Canada.

5. THE NORTHERN TERRITORIES

(Nunavut, the Northwest Territories, and Yukon)

The Northern Territories are huge in land size (one–third of Canada's land size) but small in population. Only about one hundred thousand people live there.

The Northern Territories have some unique features. A lot of the land is tundra. The land there is always frozen and there are no trees. The winters are long and cold, and in the summer the daylight can sometimes last for twenty–four hours. The north is often referred to as "the land of the midnight sun."

Multiple-Choice Questions – Chapter 19

1. What is the population of Canada?

    a) 340 million

    b) 24 million

    c) 38 million

    d) 35 million

2. Which three oceans surround Canada?

    a) The Pacific, Arctic, and Atlantic

    b) The Pacific, Arctic, and Bering

    c) The Arctic, Atlantic, and Bering

    d) The Arctic, Atlantic, and Indian

3. How many provinces does Canada have?

    a) 13

    b) 10

    c) 9

    d) 15

4. What is the national capital of Canada?

    a) Toronto

    b) Hamilton

    c) Vancouver

    d) Ottawa

5. How many regions are there in Canada?

    a) 4

    b) 10

    c) 5

    d) 6

6. What is not a region of Canada?

    a) The Prairie Provinces

    b) The Atlantic Region

    c) The Central Plains

    d) The Northern Territories

Review Questions – Chapter 19

1. What is the Canadian Shield?

2. How many provinces and territories are there in Canada?

3. What are the five regions of Canada?

4. What region accounts for more than 50 percent of Canada's population?

5. What region is famous for farming and energy resources?

6. What region only has a population of about one hundred thousand?

7. What region is bordered by the Pacific Ocean?

8. What region is on the east coast of Canada?

Chapter 20

THE PROVINCES

Here are some key facts about Canada's ten provinces:

BRITISH COLUMBIA

- Victoria is the capital of B.C.

- Four million people live in B.C.

- Vancouver is the most populated city in B.C. and is "the gateway to the Asia–Pacific."

- After English, Chinese dialects and Punjabi are the most commonly spoken languages.

- The Okanagan Valley in B.C. is famous for its fruit and wine industry.

- B.C. has the most valuable forestry industry.

ALBERTA

- Edmonton is the capital of Alberta.

- Alberta is famous for its natural beauty and is the most populated prairie province.

- The Rocky Mountains, Lake Louise, and Banff National Park are popular tourist destinations.

- The oil sands in Alberta produce the most oil and gas in Canada.

- The Badlands of Alberta are famous for dinosaur fossils.

- Alberta is also one the biggest beef producers in the world.

SASKATCHEWAN

- Regina is the capital of Saskatchewan.

- Saskatoon is the largest city in Saskatchewan.

- Saskatchewan is most famous for its agriculture (wheat and oilseeds) and mining (potash and uranium).

- Saskatchewan is often called "the breadbasket of the world."

MANITOBA

- Winnipeg is the capital of Manitoba.

- The French Quarter in Winnipeg (called St. Boniface) is the largest French–speaking community in Western Canada.

- Manitoba has a larger Aboriginal population than any other province (over 15 percent).

- Fourteen percent of Manitobans claim Ukrainian ancestry.

- Portage and Main, found in Winnipeg, is the most famous street intersection in Canada.

ONTARIO

- Toronto is the capital of Ontario and also the largest city in Canada.

- Toronto is also the financial hub of Canada.

- Over thirteen million people live in Ontario.

- Ontario was founded by the United Empire Loyalists.

- Canada's capital city, Ottawa, is also in Ontario.

- Four of the five Great Lakes are found in Ontario (Lake Erie, Lake Ontario, Lake Huron, and Lake Superior).

- The largest Francophone community outside of Quebec is found in Ontario.

- Ontario produces fruit, wine, beef, poultry, vegetables, and grains.

QUEBEC

- Quebec City is the capital of Quebec.

- Montreal is the largest city in Quebec and the second largest city in Canada.

- Montreal is the second largest French–speaking city in the world.

- Eight million people live in the province of Quebec.

- Seventy–five percent of the population speaks French as their first language.

- Quebec is the biggest producer of hydroelectricity in Canada.

- Forestry, mining, pharmaceuticals, and aeronautics are other important industries.

NEW BRUNSWICK

- Fredericton is the capital of New Brunswick.

- St. John is the largest city in N.B.

- Moncton is the French/Acadian centre of N.B.

- The Appalachian Mountains run through N.B.

- New Brunswick was founded by the United Empire Loyalists.

- New Brunswick is the only officially bilingual province.

- Mining, fishing, agriculture, forestry, and tourism are important industries.

NOVA SCOTIA

- Halifax is the capital of Nova Scotia.
- The highest tides of the world are found at the Bay of Fundy in N.S.
- Nova Scotia is well known for shipbuilding.
- Halifax is the largest port on the east coast (important for trade and defence).
- Nova Scotia has strong Celtic and Gaelic roots.
- The military tattoo is an important festival in N.S.

PRINCE EDWARD ISLAND

- Charlottetown is the capital of P.E.I.
- P.E.I. is the smallest province in Canada and is the birthplace of Confederation.
- P.E.I. is well known for its red sand beaches, potatoes, and *Anne of Green Gables* (a book by Lucy Maud Montgomery).
- The Confederation Bridge, which joins P.E.I. to mainland Canada, is a long multi–span bridge.

NEWFOUNDLAND AND LABRADOR

- St. John's is the capital of Newfoundland and Labrador.
- Newfoundland and Labrador was the last province to join Canada in 1949.
- Newfoundland and Labrador is well known for its fishing, offshore oil and gas, hydroelectric, and forestry industries.
- Newfoundland and Labrador is also the oldest colony of the British Empire.
- Newfoundland and Labrador is the easternmost point in Canada.

The Territories

Here are some key facts about Canada's three territories:

NUNAVUT

- Iqaluit is the capital of Nunavut.

- It was formed in 1999 and is Canada's newest territory.

- Inuktitut is the official language (85 percent of the population is Inuit).

- Nunavut has a nineteen–member Legislative Assembly.

- Martin Frobisher was a famous explorer who charted the Arctic for Queen Elizabeth I of England in 1576.

NORTHWEST TERRITORIES

- Yellowknife (population twenty thousand) is the capital of N.W.T.

- Yellowknife is often called "the diamond capital of North America."

- N.W.T has a large Dene, Inuit, and Metis population (more than half).

- The longest river in Canada, the Mackenzie River (forty–two hundred km) is in the N.W.T. The Mackenzie River is the second longest river in North America.

- The N.W.T was formed by merging Rupert's Land and the North Western Territory in 1870.

YUKON

- Whitehorse is the capital of Yukon.

- The lowest temperature ever recorded in Yukon (and in Canada) was −63°C.

- In the 1890s, there was a famous gold rush in Yukon.

- Mining is still an important part of Yukon's economy.

- A train trip from Skagway in Alaska to Whitehorse is an old but still popular tourist destination, due to its beautiful scenery.

- Mount Logan, the highest mountain in Canada, is in Yukon. It was named after Sir William Logan, who was a famous geologist in Canada.

The Capital Cities of Canada

British Columbia – Victoria

Alberta – Edmonton

Saskatchewan – Regina

Manitoba – Winnipeg

Ontario – Toronto

Quebec – Quebec City

New Brunswick – Fredericton

Nova Scotia – Halifax

Prince Edward Island – Charlottetown

Newfoundland and Labrador – St. John's

Yukon – Whitehorse

Northwest Territories – Yellowknife

Nunavut – Iqaluit

Multiple-Choice Questions – Chapter 20

1. Toronto is the capital city of which province?

    a) Manitoba

    b) Alberta

    c) British Columbia

    d) Ontario

2. What is the capital city of British Columbia?

    a) Vancouver

    b) Toronto

    c) Montreal

    d) Victoria

3. Regina is the capital city of which province?

    a) Manitoba

    b) Alberta

    c) Saskatchewan

    d) New Brunswick

4. What is the capital city of Prince Edward Island?

    a) Fredericton

    b) Quebec City

    c) Halifax

    d) Charlottetown

5. Where is Fredericton?

    a) Newfoundland and Labrador

    b) New Brunswick

    c) British Columbia

    d) Prince Edward Island

6. What is the capital of Nunavut?

    a) Whitehorse

    b) Yellowknife

    c) Iqaluit

    d) Winnipeg

7. Which is the smallest province in Canada?

    a) Saskatchewan

    b) Nova Scotia

    c) Nunavut

    d) Prince Edward Island

8. Which is the only officially bilingual province in Canada?

    a) Quebec

    b) Ontario

    c) New Brunswick

    d) Nova Scotia

9. Where is Mount Logan located?

    a) Yukon

    b) Nunavut

    c) Northwest Territories

    d) Ontario

10. Which province is the biggest producer of hydroelectricity in Canada?

    a) Yukon

    b) Manitoba

    c) British Columbia

    d) Quebec

11. What is the official language of Nunavut?

    a) Punjabi

    b) Inuit

    c) Inuktitut

    d) French

12. Which was the last province to join Canada in 1949?

    a) Nunavut

    b) Newfoundland and Labrador

    c) Manitoba

    d) Nova Scotia

Review Questions – Chapter 20

1. Which territory had a famous gold rush in the 1890s?

2. What is the capital of Newfoundland and Labrador?

3. Which province is connected to mainland Canada by the Confederation Bridge?

4. What is the most famous intersection in Canada?

5. Where is Yellowknife?

6. Where are the highest tides in the world?

7. Which province is known as the birthplace of Confederation?

8. Which province is often referred to as *the breadbasket of the world*?

9. Where are the oil sands?

10. Which province has the largest Francophone community outside of Quebec?

Chapter 21

THE ANTHEMS OF CANADA

The national anthem of Canada is called "**O Canada.**" It became the national anthem in **1980. The royal anthem** of Canada is called "**God Save the Queen.**" Both anthems have English and French translations.

Below are the lyrics to "O Canada" in English and French:

O Canada!
Our home and native land!
True patriot love in all thy sons command.
With glowing hearts we see thee rise,
The True North strong and free!
From far and wide,
O Canada, we stand on guard for thee.
God keep our land glorious and free!
O Canada, we stand on guard for thee.
O Canada, we stand on guard for thee.

O Canada! Terre de nos aïeux,
Ton front est ceint de fleurons glorieux!
Car ton bras sait porter l'épée,
Il sait porter la croix!
Ton histoire est une épopée
Des plus brillants exploits.
Et ta valeur, de foi trempée,
Protégera nos foyers et nos droits.
Protégera nos foyers et nos droits.

Awards in Canada

In 1967, the Order of Canada was created to honour and respect extraordinary Canadians.

The Victoria Cross is the highest level of honour (or award) that a Canadian can receive. Since 1854, ninety–six people have received the Victoria Cross for their bravery or service.

Here are some famous Victoria Cross recipients:

Lieutenant Alexander Roberts Dunn, the very first person to receive the Victoria Cross, fought in the Crimean War.

Able Seaman William Hall fought in the Siege of Lucknow in the Indian Rebellion of 1857. Hall was the first black recipient of the Victoria Cross.

Corporal Filip Konowal fought in the battle of the Hill 70 in 1917.

Billy Bishop received the Victoria Cross for his amazing piloting skills in World War I. He was known as the "Flying Ace."

Captain Paul Triquet led a famous attack on Casa Berardi in Italy during World War II.

Important Dates in Canada

Below are some important dates in Canada that are unique to Canadian history and heritage:

- Sir John A. Macdonald Day – January 11

- Vimy Day – April 9

- Victoria Day – Monday before May 25 (national holiday)

- Fete Nationale (St. Jean Baptiste Day) – June 24 (only celebrated in Quebec)

- Canada Day – July 1 (national holiday)

- Labour Day – The first Monday of September

- Remembrance Day – November 11 (national holiday)

- Sir Wilfred Laurier Day – November 20 (Sir Wilfred Laurier was Canada's first French Canadian Prime Minister. His picture is on the five–dollar bill)

Multiple-Choice Questions – Chapter 21

1. What is the royal anthem of Canada?

   a) "O Canada"

   b) "The Maple Leaf Forever"

   c) "God Save the Queen"

   d) "The True North"

2. When did "O Canada" become the national anthem?

   a) 1969

   b) 1980

   c) 1982

   d) 1867

3. What is the highest level of honour a Canadian can receive?

   a) The Grey Cup

   b) The Elizabeth Cross

   c) The Nobel Prize

   d) The Victoria Cross

4. Who was the first to receive the Victoria Cross?

   a) Billy Bishop

   b) Lieutenant Alexander Roberts Dunn

   c) Captain Paul Triquet

   d) Corporal Filip Konowal

5. When is Canada Day?

    a) April 9

    b) November 11

    c) May 24

    d) July 1

6. What is November 11 known as?

    a) Sir John A. Macdonald Day

    b) Remembrance Day

    c) Victoria Day

    d) Sir Wilfred Laurier Day

Review Questions – Chapter 21

1. What is the national anthem of Canada?

2. When was the Order of Canada established?

3. Who was the first black recipient of the Victoria Cross?

4. Who was Billy Bishop?

5. When is Victoria Day?

6. When is Sir John A. Macdonald Day?

ANSWER KEY

Multiple-Choice Questions – Chapter 1

1. What sources do the laws of Canada come from?

   a) English common law

   b) France's civil code

   c) Great Britain's constitution

   d) **All of the above**

2. What is a freedom that we do *not* enjoy in Canada?

   a) Freedom of peaceful assembly

   b) Freedom of conscience and religion

   c) **Freedom to carry weapons**

   d) Freedom of association

3. What was added to the Canadian Constitution in 1982?

   a) The Quebec Act

   b) The Treaty of Versailles

   c) **The Canadian Charter of Rights and Freedoms**

   d) The North American Free Trade Agreement

4. What are *mobility rights*?

   a) The right to leave and enter Canada anytime

   b) The right to move to any province

   c) The right to work anywhere in Canada

   d) **All of the above**

5. What freedom or right is not included in the Canadian Charter of Rights and Freedoms?

   a) Aboriginal Peoples' Rights

   b) **Discrimination Rights**

   c) Official Language Rights

   d) Multiculturalism

6. What are the official languages of Canada?

   a) English and in some situations French

   b) English, French, and Inuktitut

   c) English, French, and the Aboriginal languages

   d) **English and French**

7. Are immigrants expected to follow the laws of Canada?

    a) **Yes**

    b) No

    c) Yes, but only if they do not conflict with their own cultural beliefs

    d) Sometimes

8. What is not an example of a responsibility a Canadian must assume?

    a) Serving on a jury

    b) Voting in elections

    c) Helping people in your community

    d) **Joining the military**

9. What statement is true?

    a) Judges are above the law

    b) **No one is above the law**

    c) The RCMP has special privileges within the laws of Canada

    d) The Prime Minister cannot be arrested

10. What is the name of the military in Canada?

    a) The Canadian Federal Police

    b) **The Canadian Forces**

    c) The Toronto Maple Leafs

    d) The Royal Canadian Mounted Police

11. Is military service mandatory in Canada?

    a) **No**

    b) Yes

    c) Only for men

    d) Only for students between the ages of 18 and 20

12. Who helps keep Canada's north safe?

    a) The O.P.P.

    b) The Hamilton Tiger–Cats

    c) **The Canadian Rangers**

    d) The Nunavut Tundra Patrol

Multiple-Choice Questions – Chapter 2

1. What is Canada also known as?

   a) The Great White North

   b) **The Great Dominion**

   c) The Northern Territories

   d) Prince Rupert's Land

2. What Act formed the Confederation of Canada?

   a) The British North America Act of 1887

   b) The Quebec Act of 1774

   c) **The British North America Act of 1867**

   d) The Constitution Act of 1982

3. Who are the three founding peoples of Canada?

   a) French, British, and Vikings

   b) First Nations, Inuit, and Metis

   c) Acadian, French, and Aboriginal

   d) **Aboriginal, French, and British**

4. Where did the Canadian government put many Aboriginal children from the 1800s until the 1980s?

   a) Reserves

   b) **Residential schools**

   c) The Northern Territories

   d) Larger municipalities

5. What are the three main groups of Aboriginal peoples in Canada?

   a) First Nations, Inuit, and Acadian

   b) Algonquin, Dene, and Inuit

   c) **Inuit, Metis, and First Nations**

   d) Acadian, Inuit, and Metis

6. What is the smallest group of Aboriginal People's in Canada?

   a) **Inuit**

   b) First Nations

   c) Metis

7. What is the only officially bilingual province in Canada?

   a) Ontario

   b) Quebec

   c) **New Brunswick**

   d) Nova Scotia

8. Who are the Acadians?

   a) An ethnic group that resides in British Columbia

   b) **Descendants of early French settlers**

   c) English–speaking Quebecers

   d) A group of people descended from early Norse settlers

9. Who are the Quebecers?

   a) **The people of Quebec**

   b) Francophones

   c) Anglophones

   d) Acadians

10. What is an Anglophone?

    a) A person who speaks English as a second language

    b) A French speaker

    c) A bilingual person

    d) **A person who speaks English as a first language**

11. What is the largest religious denomination in Canada?

    a) Muslim

    b) **Catholic**

    c) Protestant

    d) Sikh

12. After English and French, what language(s) are spoken the most in Canada?

    a) Spanish

    b) Arabic

    c) **Chinese languages**

    d) Punjabi

1. Who were the first Europeans to reach Canada?

    a) The Spanish

    b) The French

    c) The British

    d) **The Vikings**

2. Which explorer was the first to draw a map of Canada's east coast?

    a) King Charles II

    b) Jacques Cartier

    c) **John Cabot**

    d) Samuel de Champlain

3. What explorer heard the Iroquian word *kanata*?

    a) Jacques Cartier

    b) Samuel de Champlain

    c) John Cabot

    d) King Charles II

4. Who founded Quebec City in 1608?

    a) Jacques Cartier

    b) John Cabot

    c) John Graves Simcoe

    d) **Samuel de Champlain**

5. Which two groups made peace in 1701?

    a) The French and the British

    b) **The French and the Iroquois**

    c) The British and the Huron

    d) The Huron and the Iroquois

6. What were the French settlements North America called?

    a) **Royal New France**

    b) Quebec

    c) Stadacona

    d) Acadia

7. What animal was central to the success of the fur trade?

   a) Mink

   b) Fox

   c) Caribou

   d) **Beaver**

8. What company was granted all of the land around the Hudson Bay to hunt and trade in 1670?

   a) Eaton's

   b) **The Hudson's Bay Company**

   c) The Quebec Fur exchange

   d) Tim Hortons

9. Who were the *coureur des bois* and the *voyageurs*?

   a) French soldiers

   b) British fur–trading workers

   c) Aboriginal hunters employed by the Hudson's Bay Company

   d) **French fur traders and fur transporters**

10. What Hudson's Bay Company trading post eventually became Winnipeg?

    a) Fort Niagara

    b) Fort George

    c) Fort Langley

    d) **Fort Garry**

11. What battle happened in 1759 between the French and the British?

    a) **The Battle of the Plains of Abraham**

    b) The Battle of Beaver Dams

    c) The Battle of Vimy Ridge

    d) The Battle of Stadacona

12. Which two commanders fought at the Battle of the Plains of Abraham?

    a) Brigadier James Wolfe and Count Frontenac

    b) **Brigadier James Wolfe and Marquis de Montcalm**

    c) Sir Guy Carleton and the Duke of Wellington

    d) Marquis de Montcalm and Sir Isaac Brock

Multiple-Choice Questions – Chapter 4

1. After the Battle of the Plains of Abraham, what was the French colony renamed?

a) Ontario

b) **Province of Quebec**

c) Nova Scotia

d) Montreal

2. What act in 1774 allowed the French to keep their identity and culture?

a) **The Quebec Act**

b) The Constitutional Act

c) The British North America Act

d) The French Constitution Act

3. Who were the *Canadiens* and the *habitants*?

a) British and French settlers living in Quebec

b) British settlers living in the new Province of Quebec

c) Employees of the Fur Trade

d) **The French–speaking Catholics of Quebec**

4. Who were the United Empire Loyalists?

a) Immigrants who left Canada to join the American Revolution

b) Immigrants who relocated to Ontario from Quebec

c) Immigrants who remained loyal to Royal New France

d) **Immigrants who came to Canada during the American Revolution because they supported the British Crown**

5. How many Loyalists came to Quebec and Nova Scotia during the American Revolution?

a) **About 40,000**

b) About 4,000

c) About 400,000

d) About 400

6. Who was Joseph Brant?

a) A Metis leader

b) **A Mohawk Indian leader**

c) A Inuit leader

d) A French Canadian leader

7. What did the British Parliament pass in 1791?

   a) The Constitution Act

   b) **The Constitutional Act**

   c) The Quebec Act

   d) The British North America Act

8. What did the Constitutional Act create?

   a) Quebec and New Brunswick

   b) Ontario, Quebec, and Nova Scotia

   c) Upper Canada and New Brunswick

   d) **Upper Canada and Lower Canada**

9. In what year was the first representative assembly elected in Nova Scotia?

   a) 1833

   b) 1812

   c) **1758**

   d) 1793

10. Who helped abolish slavery in Upper Canada in 1793?

    a) Sir John A. Macdonald

    b) The Duke of Wellington

    c) **John Graves Simcoe**

    d) Mary Ann Shad

11. When did British Parliament abolish slavery throughout the whole empire?

    a) **1833**

    b) 1823

    c) 1791

    d) 1812

12. What was the name of the secret network that helped black slaves escape to British North America?

    a) The Freedom Passage

    b) **The Underground Railroad**

    c) The Railroad of Freedom

    d) The Tunnel to Canada

1. Who invaded British North America (Canada) in 1812?

    a) France

    b) **The United States**

    c) Spain

    d) Belgium

2. Who was Chief Tecumseh?

    a) An American military general

    b) A Canadian militiaman

    c) **A famous Shawnee leader**

    d) A Quebecois brigadier general

3. Who travelled 30 km by foot to warn the British that the Americans were planning an attack in 1813?

    a) Major–General Sir Isaac Brock

    b) The Duke of Wellington

    c) Lieutenant James Fitzgibbon

    d) **Laura Secord**

4. What did Major General Robert Ross and a British force burn down in 1814?

    a) The Parliament buildings

    b) Fort York

    c) Fort George

    d) **The White House**

5. What is the former name of Toronto?

    a) Bytown

    b) **York**

    c) Stadacona

    d) Hamilton

6. What happened in Toronto and near Montreal between 1837 and 1838?

    a) A flu epidemic

    b) An American invasion

    c) A great fire

    d) **Rebellions**

7. What happened to the Rebellions of 1837–1838?

    a) The rebels overthrew the government

    b) **The rebels were defeated**

    c) The rebels escaped to Europe

    d) The rebels captured the Parliament buildings

8. Who suggested that Upper Canada and Lower Canada be united in 1840?

    a) **Lord Durham**

    b) Robert Baldwin

    c) Sir George–Etienne Cartier

    d) Joseph Howe

9. What was the name of the new province that was formed by the joining of Upper and Lower Canada?

    a) Prince Rupert's land

    b) The Province of Quebec

    c) **The Province of Canada**

    d) The Province of Ontario

10. What kind of government did Lord Durham recommend in Canada?

    a) Parliamentary democracy

    b) **Responsible government**

    c) A dictatorship

    d) Representational democracy

11. Who became the head of the first *responsible government* in Canada in 1849?

    a) **Sir Louis–Hippolyte La Fontaine**

    b) Sir John A. Macdonald

    c) Lord Durham

    d) Robert Baldwin

12. What position is this similar to in today's government?

    a) The Premier

    b) The Governor General

    c) **The Prime Minister**

    d) The Lieutenant Governor

1. What act was passed on July 1, 1867?

    a) The Quebec Act

    b) The Constitutional Act

    c) The British North America Act

    d) The Confederation Act

2. Who first mentioned the *Dominion of Canada*?

    a) Joseph Howe

    b) Sir George–Etienne Cartier

    c) Sir Leonard Tilley

    d) Sir John A. Macdonald

3. What holiday do Canadians celebrate on July 1?

    a) Victoria Day

    b) Canada Day

    c) Independence Day

    d) Remembrance Day

4. What were the first four provinces of the Confederation?

    a) Ontario, New Brunswick, Nova Scotia, and P.E.I.

    b) Ontario, Quebec, Nova Scotia, and P.E.I.

    c) Quebec, Nova Scotia, Ontario, and New Brunswick

    d) Quebec, P.E.I., Nova Scotia, and New Brunswick

5. Who became the first Prime Minister of Canada?

    a) Louis Riel

    b) George–Etienne Cartier

    c) Leonard Tilley

    d) John A. Macdonald

6. What was the last province to join the Confederation of Canada?

    a) Manitoba

    b) Newfoundland and Labrador

    c) Nunavut

    d) British Columbia

1. Who is the *Father of Manitoba*?

    a) Gabriel Dumont

    b) Sir John A. Macdonald

    c) **Louis Riel**

    d) Lord Stratchona

2. What aboriginal group did Louis Riel belong to?

    a) **Metis**

    b) Inuit

    c) First Nations

    d) Dene

3. What fort did Riel and his supporters seize in 1869?

    a) Fort York

    b) Fort Henry

    c) Fort George

    d) **Fort Garry**

4. What police force did Sir John A. Macdonald create in 1873?

    a) Royal Canadian Mounted Police

    b) **North West Mounted Police**

    c) Ontario Provincial Police

    d) Canadian Security Intelligence Service

5. Who was a great Metis military leader?

    a) Sir John A. Macdonald

    b) Sir Sam Steele

    c) Lord Strathcona

    d) **Gabriel Dumont**

6. What happened to Louis Riel?

    a) **He was executed for treason**

    b) He escaped to the United States

    c) He was killed during the Red River Rebellions

    d) He became the Premier of Manitoba

7. In what year was the Canadian Pacific Railway completed?

    a) 1875

    b) **1885**

    c) 1867

    d) 1895

8. What province agreed to join Confederation if the railway was completed?

    a) **British Columbia**

    b) Saskatchewan

    c) Manitoba

    d) Alberta

9. What was the Canadian Pacific Railway a symbol of?

    a) Economic strength

    b) **Canadian unity**

    c) Peace

    d) The lumber industry

10. Who drove in the last spike in the Canadian Pacific Railway?

    a) **Lord Strathcona**

    b) Sir John A. Macdonald

    c) Sir Sanford Fleming

    d) Sir Arthur Currie

11. What immigrant group helped build the Canadian Pacific Railway?

    a) Polish

    b) Italian

    c) Irish

    d) **Chinese**

12. What discriminatory tax did many Chinese immigrants face after the railway was completed?

    a) The H.S.T.

    b) **The Head Tax**

    c) The Visa Tax

    d) The G.S.T.

1. How many soldiers did Canada supply in World War I?

   a) About 40,000
   b) **More than 600,000**
   c) 8 million
   d) 3,000

2. How many Canadian *Bluebird* nurses helped in World War I?

   a) Around 5,000
   b) About 1,000
   c) More than 7,000
   d) **More than 3,000**

3. How many Canadian soldiers were killed or injured during the Battle of Vimy Ridge?

   a) **10,000**
   b) 1,000
   c) 100,000
   d) 50,000

4. When is Vimy Day?

   a) March 3
   b) November 11
   c) **April 9**
   d) May 24

5. Who was Canada's greatest soldier in World War I?

   a) **Sir Arthur Currie**
   b) Sir Sam Steele
   c) Phil Edwards
   d) John McCrae

6. When is Remembrance Day observed?

   a) June 24
   b) January 11
   c) April 9
   d) **November 11**

7. What do Canadians wear on Remembrance Day?

   a) A white lily

   b) **A red poppy**

   c) A red rose

   d) A red maple leaf

8. Who wrote "In Flanders Fields"?

   a) Arthur Currie

   b) Rohinton Mistry

   c) Margaret Atwood

   d) **John McCrae**

9. How many Canadian soldiers died in World War I?

   a) 80,000

   b) 600,000

   c) **60,000**

   d) 40,000

10. What Canadian province became the first to let women vote?

    a) Ontario

    b) **Manitoba**

    c) British Columbia

    d) Quebec

11. Who led the women's suffrage movement in Canada?

    a) **Dr. Emily Stowe**

    b) Agnes Macphail

    c) Kim Campbell

    d) Adrienne Clarkson

12. Who became Canada's first female MP?

    a) Roberta Borden

    b) Lucy Maud Montgomery

    c) Dr. Emily Stowe

    d) **Agnes Macphail**

1. When did Canada join World War II?

    a) 1935

    b) **1939**

    c) 1918

    d) 1945

2. How many Canadians and Newfoundlanders served in World War II?

    a) About 10,000

    b) About 100,000

    c) **More than 1 million**

    d) About half a million

3. When was D–Day?

    a) September 3, 1945

    b) November 11, 1944

    c) November 11, 1945

    d) **June 6, 1944**

4. When did Germany surrender?

    a) **May 8, 1945**

    b) November 11, 1945

    c) June 6, 1945

    d) June 6, 1944

5. How many Canadian soldiers were killed in World War II?

    a) 33,000

    b) 400,000

    c) **44,000**

    d) 80,000

6. When did the Government of Canada apologize to Japanese Canadians for the mistreatment they endured during World War II?

    a) 2006

    b) 1996

    c) 2008

    d) **1988**

1. What valuable resource was discovered in Alberta in 1947?

    a) Dinosaur fossils

    b) **Oil**

    c) Gold

    d) Uranium

2. What year was Employment Insurance introduced?

    a) 1950

    b) 1949

    c) **1940**

    d) 1969

3. When was the Canadian Pension Plan introduced?

    a) **1965**

    b) 1940

    c) 1939

    d) 1945

4. What organizations has Canada joined?

    a) NATO

    b) NORAD

    c) UN

    d) **All of the above**

5. How many Canadians died in the Korean War?

    a) 300

    b) 100

    c) 1,000

    d) **500**

6. When were Aboriginal people granted the right to vote?

    a) 1945

    b) 1970

    c) 1948

    d) **1960**

7. What were the changes that happened in Quebec during the 1960s known as?

    a) The Noise Movement

    b) The Calm Storm

    c) The Silent Rebellion

    d) **The Quiet Revolution**

8. What act declared that English and French would be offered for all federal services?

    a) The Constitution Act

    b) **The Official Languages Act**

    c) The Official Bilingual Act

    d) The Quebec Act

9. When was *La Francophonie* founded?

    a) 1975

    b) 1965

    c) 1960

    d) **1970**

10. In which two years did Quebec hold a referendum?

    a) 1980 and 1985

    b) 1983 and 1985

    c) **1980 and 1995**

    d) 1990 and 1995

Multiple-Choice Questions – Chapter 11

1. Who are two famous Canadian writers?

    a) Robertson Davies and Oscar Peterson

    b) Robertson Davies and Healey Willan

    c) **Margaret Laurence and Mordecai Richler**

    d) Margaret Laurence and Emily Carr

2. Who is a famous Canadian musician?

    a) Pauline Johnson

    b) Robertson Davies

    c) Joy Kagawa

    d) **Oscar Peterson**

3. Who was the *Group of Seven*?

    a) **A group of landscape painters**

    b) A group of poets

    c) A Canadian jazz band

    d) A group of Inuit sculptors

4. Who is a famous Inuit artist?

    a) **Kenojuak Ashevak**

    b) Denys Arcand

    c) Jean–Paul Riopelle

    d) Emily Carr

5. Who is Atom Egoyan?

    a) A writer

    b) A painter

    c) **A filmmaker**

    d) A sculptor

6. Who is famous for painting totem poles on the West Coast of Canada?

    a) Jean–Paul Riopelle

    b) **Emily Carr**

    c) Denys Arcand

    d) Robertson Davies

7. What is Canada's official winter sport?

    a) Lacrosse

    b) Basketball

    c) **Hockey**

    d) Football

8. What do teams in the CFL try to win?

    a) The Clarkson Cup

    b) The Stanley Cup

    c) **The Grey Cup**

    d) The Ryder Cup

9. Who invented basketball in 1891?

    a) **James Naismith**

    b) Lord Grey

    c) Mark Tewksbury

    d) Terry Fox

10. Who started *the Marathon of Hope* in 1980?

    a) Donovan Bailey

    b) **Terry Fox**

    c) Catriona Le May Doan

    d) James Naismith

11. Who scored the winning goal in the famous 1972 hockey game against the Soviet Union at the Olympics?

    a) **Paul Henderson**

    b) Wayne Gretzky

    c) Sidney Crosby

    d) Donovan Bailey

12. What is Canada's official summer sport?

    a) Football

    b) Baseball

    c) Hockey

    d) **Lacrosse**

Multiple-Choice Questions – Chapter 12

1. What huge mechanical arm invented by SPAR was used by NASA for thirty years?

    a) The Manitobarm

    b) **The Canadarm**

    c) The Canadian Elbow

    d) The Hubble telescope

2. Who is a Canadian Nobel Prize winner?

    a) Sir Sanford Fleming

    b) Robertson Davies

    c) Louis–Phillippe Hebert

    d) **John Polanyi**

3. Who discovered insulin?

    a) Sir Frederick Banting and Matthew Evans

    b) Alexander Graham Bell

    c) Matthew Evans and Henry Woodward

    d) **Sir Frederick Banting and Charles Best**

4. What did Alexander Graham Bell develop?

    a) The radio

    b) The pacemaker

    c) The telephone

    d) The snowmobile

5. Who developed the Standard Time Zone system?

    a) Sir Sanford Fleming

    b) Joseph–Armand Bombardier

    c) Matthew Evans and Henry Woodward

    d) Charles Best

6. What product is RIM famous for?

    a) The blueberry

    b) The smartphone

    c) The pager

    d) The Blackberry

Multiple-Choice Questions – Chapter 13

1. What is an important fact about the Canadian government?

    a) It is a constitutional monarchy

    b) It is a federal state

    c) It is a parliamentary democracy

    d) All of the above

2. What level of government is responsible for *citizenship*?

    a) The municipal level

    b) The federal level

    c) The provincial level

    d) All of the above

3. What are the three parts of Parliament?

    a) The Senate, the Sovereign, and the Prime Minister

    b) The House of Commons, the Lieutenant Governor, and the Senate

    c) The House of Commons, the Senate, and the Sovereign

    d) The Prime Minister, the Senate, and the Sovereign

4. Who is the *head of state* in Canada?

   a) The president

   b) The Prime Minister

   c) **The Queen or King of England**

   d) The Governor General

5. Who represents the Sovereign in Canada?

   a) **The Governor General**

   b) The Lieutenant General

   c) The Prime Minister

   d) The Senate

6. Who represents the Sovereign in the provinces?

   a) A senator

   b) **A Lieutenant Governor**

   c) A commissioner

   d) A member of Parliament

Multiple-Choice Questions – Chapter 14

1. What are the three levels of government?

   a) Federal, provincial, and state

   b) Federal, electoral district, and municipality

   c) Federal, parliamentary, and municipal

   d) **Federal, provincial (or territorial), and municipal**

2. Where does the federal government meet?

   a) **In the Parliament buildings in Ottawa**

   b) At Queen's Park in Toronto

   c) In Ottawa's city hall

   d) In the Parliament buildings in Toronto

3. Who is the head of the federal government?

   a) The Queen

   b) **The Prime Minister**

   c) The Governor General

   d) The minister of Finance

4. Who is the head of a provincial government?

    a) The Prime Minister

    b) A mayor

    c) **A Premier**

    d) A commissioner

5. What are the three branches of government?

    a) **The executive, the legislative, and the judicial**

    b) The executive, the legislative, and the parliamentary

    c) The legislative, the judicial, and the disciplinary

    d) The executive, the police force, and the judicial

6. What is a *law* called before it is official?

    a) **A bill**

    b) A pre–law

    c) An amendment

    d) A legislature

Multiple-Choice Questions – Chapter 15

1. Federal elections are held on the third Monday in which month?

    a) **October**

    b) November

    c) September

    d) December

2. What is a *polling station*?

    a) A place where candidates can register for the election

    b) **A place where you vote**

    c) A place where MPs work

    d) A place where political debates are held

3. What is the piece of paper you vote on called?

    a) A voter's list

    b) A riding

    c) An electoral district

    d) **A ballot**

4. How many electoral districts are there in Canada?

    a) **338**

    b) 238

    c) 408

    d) 13

5. What do you call the group of politicians that control government departments?

    a) The Prime Minister

    b) The Governor General

    c) The Senate

    d) **The Cabinet**

6. What do you call the political party with the second largest number of seats in the federal government?

    a) A minority government

    b) A majority government

    c) **Her Majesty's Loyal Opposition**

    d) The official senate

Multiple-Choice Questions – Chapter 16

1. Which of the following statements is correct?

    a) **In Canada, everyone is innocent until proven guilty**

    b) In Canada, everyone is guilty until proven innocent

    c) In Canada, you do not have the right to a fair trial

    d) All of the above

2. What is the top court of Canada?

    a) Provincial Court

    b) Family Court

    c) **The Supreme Court**

    d) Small Claims Court

3. Whose role is it to settle disagreements or conflicts?

    a) The municipality's

    b) The government's

    c) The police force's

    d) **The court's**

4. Whose job is it to enforce the laws of Canada?

    a) The courts'

    b) **The police force's**

    c) The MP's

    d) The judge's

5. Who are the federal police in Canada?

    a) The OPP

    b) The NWMP

    c) **The RCMP**

    d) CSIS

6. Which two provinces have their own provincial police?

    a) Ontario and British Columbia

    b) Quebec and Manitoba

    c) Alberta and Manitoba

    d) **Ontario and Quebec**

Multiple-Choice Questions – Chapter 17

1. What is the national animal of Canada?

    a) The caribou

    b) **The beaver**

    c) The moose

    d) The polar bear

2. What is on Canada's national flag?

    a) A maple tree

    b) A beaver

    c) A pine cone

    d) **A maple leaf**

3. What symbol is on the flag of Quebec?

    a) A caribou

    b) A maple leaf

    c) **A fleur–de–lys**

    d) A rose

4. What was built at Parliament to commemorate World War I?

    a) The Senate

    b) The Centre Block

    c) The library

    d) **The Peace Tower**

5. What does Canada's motto mean?

    a) **From sea to sea**

    b) From the river to the sea

    c) Out of many, one

    d) The true north, strong and free

6. When was Canada's red and white maple leaf flag adopted as its official national flag?

    a) 1980

    b) 1916

    c) 1955

    d) **1965**

Multiple-Choice Questions – Chapter 18

1. Who is Canada's biggest trading partner?

    a) England

    b) Japan

    c) **The United States**

    d) China

2. What three countries signed the North American Free Trade Agreement in 1984?

    a) Canada, the United States, and England

    b) **Canada, the United States, and Mexico**

    c) Canada, the United States, and China

    d) Canada, England, and France

3. What are the three main types of industry in Canada?

    a) Natural resources, computer technology, and automotive

    b) Service, communications, and hydroelectricity

    c) Natural resources, service, and communications

    d) **Service, manufacturing, and natural resources**

4. What is the most popular job industry in Canada?

    a) Natural resources

    b) Manufacturing

    c) **Service**

    d) Computers

5. Is Canada part of the G8?

    a) **Yes**

    b) No

    c) Sometimes

    d) Not anymore

6. Fishing, mining, and forestry are examples of what industry?

    a) Hydroelectric

    b) **Natural resources**

    c) Manufacturing

    d) Service

Multiple-Choice Questions – Chapter 19

1. What is the population of Canada?

    a) 340 million

    b) 24 million

    c) 38 million

    d) **35 million**

2. Which three oceans surround Canada?

    a) **The Pacific, Arctic, and Atlantic**

    b) The Pacific, Arctic, and Bering

    c) The Arctic, Atlantic, and Bering

    d) The Arctic, Atlantic, and Indian

3. How many provinces does Canada have?

    a) 13

    b) **10**

    c) 9

    d) 15

4. What is the national capital of Canada?

    a) Toronto

    b) Hamilton

    c) Vancouver

    d) **Ottawa**

5. How many regions are there in Canada?

    a) 4

    b) 10

    c) **5**

    d) 6

6. What is not a region of Canada?

    a) The Prairie Provinces

    b) The Atlantic Region

    c) **The Central Plains**

    d) The Northern Territories

Multiple-Choice Questions – Chapter 20

1. Toronto is the capital city of which province?

    a) Manitoba

    b) Alberta

    c) British Columbia

    d) **Ontario**

2. What is the capital city of British Columbia?

    a) Vancouver

    b) Toronto

    c) Montreal

    d) **Victoria**

3. Regina is the capital city of which province?

    a) Manitoba

    b) Alberta

    c) **Saskatchewan**

    d) New Brunswick

4. What is the capital city of Prince Edward Island

   a) Fredericton
   b) Quebec City
   c) Halifax
   d) **Charlottetown**

5. Where is Fredericton?

   a) Newfoundland and Labrador
   b) **New Brunswick**
   c) British Columbia
   d) Prince Edward Island

6. What is the capital of Nunavut?

   a) Whitehorse
   b) Yellowknife
   c) **Iqaluit**
   d) Winnipeg

7. Which is the smallest province in Canada?

   a) Saskatchewan
   b) Nova Scotia
   c) Nunavut
   d) **Prince Edward Island**

8. Which is the only officially bilingual province in Canada?

   a) Quebec
   b) Ontario
   c) **New Brunswick**
   d) Nova Scotia

9. Where is Mount Logan located?

   a) **Yukon**
   b) Nunavut
   c) Northwest Territories
   d) Ontario

10. Which province is the biggest producer of hydroelectricity in Canada?

   a) Yukon
   b) Manitoba
   c) British Columbia
   d) **Quebec**

11. What is the official language of Nunavut?

    a) Punjabi

    b) Inuit

    c) **Inuktitut**

    d) French

12. Which was the last province to join Canada in 1949?

    a) Nunavut

    b) **Newfoundland and Labrador**

    c) Manitoba

    d) Nova Scotia

Multiple-Choice Questions – Chapter 21

1. What is the royal anthem of Canada?

    a) "O Canada"

    b) "The Maple Leaf Forever"

    c) **"God Save the Queen"**

    d) "The True North"

2. When did "O Canada" become the national anthem?

    a) 1969

    b) **1980**

    c) 1982

    d) 1867

3. What is the highest level of honour a Canadian can receive?

    a) The Grey Cup

    b) The Elizabeth Cross

    c) The Nobel Prize

    d) **The Victoria Cross**

4. Who was the first to receive the Victoria Cross?

    a) Billy Bishop

    b) **Lieutenant Alexander Roberts Dunn**

    c) Captain Paul Triquet

    d) Corporal Filip Konowal

5. When is Canada Day?

    a) April 9

    b) November 11

    c) May 24

    d) **July 1**

6. What is November 11 known as?

    a) Sir John A. Macdonald Day

    b) **Remembrance Day**

    c) Victoria Day

    d) Sir Wilfred Laurier Day

Manufactured by Amazon.ca
Bolton, ON